Sexuality in William Shakespeare's *A Midsummer Night's Dream*

Other Books in the Social Issues in Literature Series:

Colonialism in Joseph Conrad's *Heart of Darkness*
Death and Dying in the Poetry of Emily Dickinson
Democracy in the Poetry of Walt Whitman
Depression in Sylvia Plath's *The Bell Jar*
The Environment in Rachel Carson's *Silent Spring*
The Food Industry in Eric Schlosser's *Fast Food Nation*
Poverty in John Steinbeck's *The Pearl*
Race in John Howard Griffin's *Black Like Me*
Race in William Shakespeare's *Othello*
Slavery in Toni Morrison's *Beloved*
Teen Issues in S.E. Hinton's *The Outsiders*
Women's Issues in Zora Neale Hurston's *Their Eyes Were Watching God*

Social Issues in Literature

Sexuality in William Shakespeare's *A Midsummer Night's Dream*

Gary Wiener, Book Editor

GREENHAVEN PRESS
A part of Gale, Cengage Learning

GALE
CENGAGE Learning

Detroit • New York • San Francisco • New Haven, Conn • Waterville, Maine • London

Elizabeth Des Chenes, *Director, Content Strategy*
Cynthia Sanner, *Publisher*
Douglas Dentino, *Manager, New Product*

© 2014 Greenhaven Press, a part of Gale, Cengage Learning

Gale and Greenhaven Press are registered trademarks used herein under license.

For more information, contact:
Greenhaven Press
27500 Drake Rd.
Farmington Hills, MI 48331-3535
Or you can visit our Internet site at gale.cengage.com

ALL RIGHTS RESERVED.
No part of this work covered by the copyright herein may be reproduced, transmitted, stored, or used in any form or by any means graphic, electronic, or mechanical, including but not limited to photocopying, recording, scanning, digitizing, taping, Web distribution, information networks, or information storage and retrieval systems, except as permitted under Section 107 or 108 of the 1976 United States Copyright Act, without the prior written permission of the publisher.

For product information and technology assistance, contact us at

Gale Customer Support, 1-800-877-4253
For permission to use material from this text or product, submit all requests online at www.cengage.com/permissions

Further permissions questions can be emailed to permissionrequest@cengage.com

Articles in Greenhaven Press anthologies are often edited for length to meet page requirements. In addition, original titles of these works are changed to clearly present the main thesis and to explicitly indicate the author's opinion. Every effort is made to ensure that Greenhaven Press accurately reflects the original intent of the authors. Every effort has been made to trace the owners of copyrighted material.

Cover image © Lebrecht Music and Arts Photo Library/Alamy.

LIBRARY OF CONGRESS CATALOGING-IN-PUBLICATION DATA

Sexuality in William Shakespeare's A Midsummer Night's Dream / Gary Wiener, Book Editor.
　p. cm. -- (Social issues in literature)
　Includes bibliographical references and index.
　ISBN 978-0-7377-6387-4 (hardcover)
　ISBN 978-0-7377-6388-1 (pbk.)
　1. Shakespeare, William, 1564-1616. Midsummer night's dream. 2. Sex in literature. 3. Sensuality in literature. I. Wiener, Gary, editor of compilation.
　PR2827.S36 2013
　822.3'3--dc23
　　　　　　　　　　　　　　　　　　　　　　　　　　　2013004430

Printed in the United States of America
2 3 4 5 6　　　18 17 16 15 14

Contents

Introduction   9

Chronology   16

Chapter 1: Background on William Shakespeare

1. The Life of William Shakespeare   20
   Encyclopedia of World Biography

   William Shakespeare is generally acknowledged as one of the greatest writers ever. His dramatic achievement over the course of his more than twenty-year career has left a legacy that few writers can equal.

2. Shakespeare Was Knowledgeable About Sex   32
   Stanley Wells

   From the information available in Shakespeare's sonnets and in public records, biographers can infer that Shakespeare was well versed in sexual matters, including adultery, sexually transmitted diseases, and sex scandals. Though Shakespeare's canon is full of sexual references, more so than the work of many other writers, it would be a mistake to extrapolate his sexual life from his art.

Chapter 2: Sexuality in *A Midsummer Night's Dream*

1. *A Midsummer Night's Dream* Is a War Between the Sexes   47
   Ace G. Pilkington and Olga A. Pilkington

   A Midsummer Night's Dream revolves around a series of incidents where women defy men at almost every level.

2. *A Midsummer Night's Dream* Urges Brides to the Wedding Bed   53
   David Wiles

   Shakespeare's play fits into the tradition of the epithalamium, a poem written expressly for the occasion of marriage that urges new wives to perform as expected on their wedding night.

3. The Ass Motif in *The Comedy of Errors* and *A Midsummer Night's Dream* 62
Deborah Baker Wyrick

Nick Bottom's metamorphosis into a creature with an ass's head on a man's body serves as a complex metaphor of reconciliation between chaos and order.

4. *A Midsummer Night's Dream* Exposes Taboo Sexuality 88
Bruce Boehrer

A Midsummer Night's Dream exposes taboo sexuality with its illusions to cross-species eroticism and same-sex relationships.

5. Shakespeare's Defiant Daughters Affirm a New Morality 97
Diane Elizabeth Dreher

Hermia is one of many Shakespearean daughters who defy their fathers' plans, in this case for an arranged marriage, in order to forge their own identity.

6. *A Midsummer Night's Dream*: "Jack shall have Jill; / Nought shall go ill" 107
Shirley Nelson Garner

Shakespeare's happy ending comes at the expense of women, who must give in to their male counterparts' need for control and homoerotic fulfillment.

7. Productions of *A Midsummer Night's Dream* Have Evolved Over the Years 128
W. Reginald Rampone Jr.

Since the 1600s, productions of *A Midsummer Night's Dream* have become increasingly provocative and daring, and some recent versions have gone back to an all-male cast.

Chapter 3: Contemporary Perspectives on Sexuality

1. Adolescent Sexuality Is a Universal Concern 141
Monique Long

Despite cultural, religious, geographical, and racial differences, adolescents all over the world are eager to explore their sexuality, and adults are often just as eager to keep them from doing so.

2. More Grey than Gay 146
Apoorva Dutt

People are often categorized by sexual classifications, but the truth is that many men and women defy such easy classification into categories such as gay and straight.

3. What Do Men Really Want? 151
Eric Jaffe

The stereotype of the macho male who is only interested in sex is not a real reflection of masculine romantic and sexual desires.

4. Americans Are Still Not Honest About Sexuality 164
Bob Minor

Ordinary people are afraid to discuss sexuality openly and honestly in public. Therefore, politicians, preachers, and other public figures are able to bully them into believing wrongheaded ideas about sex.

5. National Sex Education Standards
Spark Controversy 169
Nirvi Shah

Up until now there have been no national standards for what children across America are taught about sex. New national standards are an attempt to regularize sex education, but such standards are proving highly controversial.

For Further Discussion	175
For Further Reading	176
Bibliography	177
Index	182

Introduction

In his landmark 1948 study of suggestive language in the Bard of Avon's writing, *Shakespeare's Bawdy*, British lexicographer Eric Partridge made a pronouncement that might surprise contemporary readers. He labeled *A Midsummer Night's Dream* William Shakespeare's "cleanest comedy" and asserted that because it was "a pretty 'safe' play," it was a favorite for use in schools.[1] Partridge was an accomplished student of language, the author of dozens of books, and an expert on slang and unconventional language. How is it, therefore, that in covering just about every example of "the sexual, the homosexual and non-sexual" naughtiness in Shakespeare's writing could Partridge find so few risqué moments in *A Midsummer Night's Dream*, a play that has since been commonly acknowledged as one of Shakespeare's truly ribald productions? Perhaps this discrepancy speaks to the difference in the way audiences viewed theater in the 1940s and in the aftermath of the sexually more permissive 1960s. Or perhaps contemporary literary critics, as noted Shakespeare scholar Alan Wells suggests, simply have dirtier minds.[2] Whichever is the case, the title of this volume, *Sexuality in William Shakespeare's A Midsummer Night's Dream*, speaks to the now common perception that Shakespeare's once sanitary 1595 comedy is now viewed as a play rife with sexual and homosexual tension and bursting with innuendo and double entendre.

Partridge's assessment that *A Midsummer Night's Dream* was not a sexual play reflected the general view of his time. Early productions of the comedy often focused on the pageantry and spectacle of that magical night in the forest, the platonic dalliance of Titania and Nick Bottom, and the wedding festivities of Theseus and Hippolyta, featuring the performance by Peter Quince's acting troupe that Puck labels the "mechanicals." The movement toward highlighting the play's sexuality began in the early 1960s with the work of a Polish critic, Jan Kott. In his book *Shakespeare Our Contemporary*, Kott included an influential chapter, "Titania and the Ass's Head," about *A Midsummer Night's Dream* that explored what he considered its undeniable and pervasive sexual and violent elements. Kott's thesis was repudiated by several subsequent critics, but eventually, his ideas began to take hold. His essay inspired many subsequent productions of the play. According to Gary Jay Williams, Kott's influence

> ... may be apparent as early as 1966 in the staging of the play by John Hancock at the Actor's Workshop in San Francisco, and the productions of [Ariane] Mnouchkine in Paris in 1968 and [Peter] Brook in 1970.... Director John Hirsch flirted lightly with Kott's reading at Stratford, Ontario, in 1968 and again at the Guthrie Theater in 1972 and 1984.... It is hard to imagine several American productions of the 1970s and 1980s without Kott: Alvin Epstein's at the Yale Repertory Theatre in 1975, Liviu Ciulei's at the Guthrie Theater in 1985, and Mark Lamos's at the Hartford Stage Company in 1988.[3]

Such productions became increasingly provocative. Williams writes that in Hancock's production, "Demetrius ... was wired with an electric codpiece that flashed to register his sexual passions."[4] Additionally, "Overt eroticism among the fairies became the trend" in the 1960s, and "in Peter Hall's 1969 film version of the play, Judi Dench's Titania was a sensuous sea queen, all but bare-bosomed in netting over a nearly transparent body stocking."[5]

In adapting *A Midsummer Night's Dream* for the Royal Shakespeare Company's 1970 production, Jan Kott's friend, director Peter Brook (who had earlier directed the highly regarded film of William Golding's *Lord of the Flies*), followed Kott's lead in emphasizing the play's sexuality. In Brook's now notorious bower scene between Bottom and Titania, "The fairies hoisted Bottom on to their shoulders; one of them thrust a muscular arm up between Bottom's legs like a grotesque phallus; Oberon swung on a rope across the stage, and the rest of the cast threw paper plates and streamers like confetti over Bottom and Titania as the [Felix] Mendelssohn "Wedding March" blared out."[6]

Brook's production was highly popular with audiences and reviewers, and, slowly, critics began to appreciate Kott's startling sexual reevaluation of the play. Renowned Shakespearean critic David Bevington, for example, wrote that although Kott may have exaggerated *A Midsummer Night's Dream*'s sexual nature, "the dark side of love is seldom very far away" and the "conflict between sexual desire and rational restraint is ... an essential tension throughout the play."[7] Bevington credited the "overheated reactions" against Kott ... "to the reluctance of most of us to give up the romanticized and sentimentalized nineteenth-century reading of the play to which Kott is addressing his attack."[8]

As might be expected, since Kott, sexual interpretations of the play have proliferated. In a 1982 article, critic David Marshall suggests that one can read "*A Midsummer Night's Dream* as a conflict between 'masculine' principles of rationality and order and 'female' principles of sexuality and passion."[9] James Calderwood in 1991 speculates about the sexual relationship of the Duke of Athens, Theseus, and his captured Amazon, Hippolyta, questioning exactly how Theseus will consummate a relationship "with this man-woman whose sexual desire is a mystery?"[10] Alan Sinfield and Arthur L. Little Jr. offer homosexual readings of the play.[11] And the title of Bruce Thomas Boehrer's 1994 essay, "Bestial Buggery in *A Midsummer Night's Dream*," pretty much speaks for itself.[12]

Despite the spate of articles and book-length studies that have followed Kott's interpretation in the late twentieth and early twenty-first century, purists remain. In his exhaustive study, *Shakespeare: The Invention of the Human*, Harold Bloom remains skeptical of sexually explicit readings and performances of the play. He writes,

> Unfortunately, every production of it that I have been able to attend has been a brutal disaster, with the exception of Peter Hall's motion picture.... The worst I can recall are Peter Brook's (1970) and Alvin Epstein's (a Yale hilarity of 1975), but I cannot be the only lover of the play who rejects the prevailing notion that sexual violence and bestiality are at the center of this humane and wise drama.... Bottom, as the play's text comically makes clear, has considerably less sexual interest in Titania than she does in him, or than many recent critics and directors have in her. Shakespeare, here and elsewhere, is bawdy but not prurient; Bottom is amiably innocent, and not very bawdy. Sex-and-violence exalters really should look elsewhere; *Titus Andronicus* would be a fine start. If Shakespeare had desired to write an orgiastic ritual, with Bottom as "this Bacchic ass of Saturnalia and carnival" (Jan Kott), we would have a different comedy. What we do have is a gentle, mild, good-natured Bottom, who is rather more inclined to the company of the elves ... than to the madly infatuated Titania.[13]

Stanley Wells writes of a time when he believed that the play "contained only one piece of bawdy, in the joke about 'French Crowns ...,'" but, Wells, adds, "That was long ago." Still, he argues that the play is "nothing like as nocent [harmful] as many modern interpreters ... allege."[14] Perhaps, but most contemporary commentators fall more in line with the following observation from Jonathan Bate, as expressed in his biographical study, *Soul of the Age: A Biography of the Mind of William Shakespeare*: "... nearly all of Shakespeare's works—his tragedies as well as his comedies and poems—are suffused with the language of sexual desire, often expressed through unremittingly bawdy wordplay...."[15]

Regarding Shakespeare's own sexual desires, there is also much debate. Some biographers and critics claim that his sonnets suggest the poet's early bisexuality. Many others refute such claims, insisting that the sonnets, like the plays, are fiction, and that the bard's sexuality cannot be extrapolated from his works. Whatever the truth is about Shakespeare's predilections, the plays make it clear that the poet was well versed in human sexuality, much as he was keenly knowledgeable about nearly everything else a man of his era could be expected to understand. Given that few substantiated facts are known about Shakespeare's life, it is difficult to say how much of the man is in his literature, but most biographers, like Bate, suggest that Shakespeare himself had a substantial sexual appetite. Perhaps the most famous anecdote that would seem to confirm Shakespeare's interest in women, as well as his adulterous ways, comes from the diary of Shakespeare's contemporary, lawyer John Manningham. As Manningham tells it, a female theatergoer was enamored of Shakespeare's lead actor, Richard Burbage, who starred in the play *Richard III*. She arranged that Burbage should visit her for an amorous tryst and that in announcing his presence, he should use the name "Richard the Third." But Shakespeare, hearing of the arrangement, visited the woman before Burbage and was with her when the tardy actor knocked at her door. According to Manningham, when Burbage sent word that "Richard the Third" had arrived, "Shakespeare caused return to be made that William the Conqueror was before Richard the Third."[16]

Like the Shakespeare of the preceding anecdote, his character, Theseus, would seem to have urgent sexual needs. When the duke opens the play by telling Hippolyta that he cannot wait until their nuptial hour, still four long days off, the reader clearly understands that it is the wedding night that most interests the duke. By act 5, scene 1, with only three hours remaining until Theseus can finally consummate his relationship, he calls for an entertainment "To wear away this long age of three hours/Between our after-supper and bedtime."[16] In his last speech of the play, Theseus bids all assembled "to bed" twice in eight lines. It is not difficult to read the real meaning of his words.

Finally, if *A Midsummer Night's Dream* is as innocent as some claim, what does one then make of the epilogue, in which Puck apologizes to the audience?

> If we shadows have offended,
>
> Think but this, and all is mended,
>
> That you have but slumber'd here
>
> While these visions did appear.[17]

Is it just the comic silliness, the donkey's head on a man, the foolishness of characters splashed with love potion, and the awkward stylings of the mechanicals for which he would "restore amends?" Or was Shakespeare aware that there was enough bawdiness, risqué humor, and innuendo to perhaps discomfort the more puritanical members of the audience? Given that there are no records of contemporary performances of *A Midsummer Night's Dream* to consult, as with almost everything else in Shakespeare's life, we are left to wonder what antics really occurred, and just how sexually graphic or benign the play was intended to be. The essays that follow argue that Shakespeare's bawdy is fully at play in *A Midsummer Night's Dream*, and that, Eric Partridge aside, the play really is as replete with sexual puns, themes, and actions as any of those—*Measure for Measure, Much Ado About Nothing*, and *The Merry Wives of Windsor*, for example—that are generally considered to be among Shakespeare's most provocative.

Notes

1. Eric Partridge, *Shakespeare's Bawdy*. Revised ed. New York: E.P. Dutton, 1969, p. 45.
2. Stanley Wells, *Looking for Sex in Shakespeare*. Cambridge, England: Cambridge University Press, 2004, p. 2.
3. Gary Jay Williams, *Our Moonlight Revels: A Midsummer Night's Dream in the Theatre*. Iowa City: University of Iowa Press, 1997, p. 215.
4. *Ibid*, p. 217.
5. *Ibid*, p. 222.
6. Roger Warren, *A Midsummer Night's Dream: Text and Performance*. New York: Palgrave Macmillan, 1983, p. 57.

Introduction

7. David Bevington, "'But We Are Spirits of Another Sort': The Dark Side of Love and Magic in *A Midsummer Night's Dream*," in *Medieval and Renaissance Studies: Proceedings of the Southeastern Institute of Medieval and Renaissance Studies, Summer 1975*. Ed. Siegfried Wenzel. Chapel Hill: University of North Carolina Press, 1978, pp. 81 and 88.

8. *Ibid*, p. 81.

9. David Marshall, "Exchanging Visions: Reading *A Midsummer Night's Dream*," *Journal of English Literary History*, vol. 49, no. 3, Autumn 1982, p. 557.

10. James L. Calderwood, "*A Midsummer Night's Dream*: Anamorphism and Theseus' Dream," *Shakespeare Quarterly*, vol. 42, no. 4, Winter 1991, p. 414.

11. Alan Sinfield, *Shakespeare, Authority, Sexuality: Unfinished Business in Cultural Materialism*. London: Routledge, 2006, and in "'A Local Habitation and a Name': Presence, Witnessing, and Queer Marriage in Shakespeare's Romantic Comedies," in *Presentism, Gender, and Sexuality in Shakespeare*. Ed. Evelyn Gajowski. New York: Palgrave Macmillan, 2009.

12. Bruce Thomas Boehrer, "Bestial Buggery in *A Midsummer Night's Dream*," in *The Production of English Renaissance Culture*. Eds. David Lee Miller, Sharon O'Dair and Harold Weber. Ithaca, NY: Cornell University Press, 1994, pp. 123–150.

13. Harold Bloom, *Shakespeare: The Invention of the Human*. New York: Riverhead, 1998, pp. 148–149.

14. Stanley Wells, *Looking for Sex in Shakespeare*. Cambridge, England: Cambridge University Press, 2004, p. 31.

15. Jonathan Bate, *Soul of the Age: A Biography of the Mind of William Shakespeare*. New York: Random House, 2009, p. 389.

16. *The Oxford Book of Literary Anecdotes*. Ed. James Sutherland. New York: Pocket Books, 1987. p. 17.

17. William Shakespeare, *A Midsummer Night's Dream*. Ed. Harold F. Brooks. London: Thomson, 2004, p. 127.

Chronology

1564
William Shakespeare is born to John and Mary Shakespeare in Stratford-upon-Avon, England.

1569
Shakespeare's father, John, is elected bailiff (mayor) of Stratford-upon-Avon.

1582
Shakespeare marries Anne Hathaway.

1583
Susanna Shakespeare, the poet's first child, is born.

1585
Twins Judith and Hamnet are born to Shakespeare and his wife.

1588–1589
Shakespeare goes to London, leaving his family behind.

1590–1593
Shakespeare writes his early plays, which are performed for the first time, including *The Comedy of Errors, Titus Andronicus,* and *Richard III.*

1594
Romeo and Juliet is first performed. Shakespeare's acting troupe becomes the Lord Chamberlain's Men and performs for Queen Elizabeth.

1595
A Midsummer Night's Dream is first performed.

1596

Shakespeare's son, Hamnet, dies.

1597

Henry IV, Part I is first performed.

1599

The Globe Theatre is built in London. *Henry V, As You Like It,* and *Julius Caesar* are performed.

1600

Hamlet is performed. The first edition of *A Midsummer Night's Dream* is published.

1601

Shakespeare's father, John, dies.

1603

Queen Elizabeth dies. James I ascends the English throne. Shakespeare's troupe becomes the King's Men, and it performs for the royal court.

1603–1606

Shakespeare's great tragedies *Othello, Macbeth,* and *King Lear* are written and performed.

1609

Shakespeare's sonnets are published.

1609–1611

The late romances *Cymbeline, The Winter's Tale,* and *The Tempest* are performed.

ca. 1612

Shakespeare retires from the stage.

1613
The Globe Theatre burns down.

1614
The Globe Theatre is rebuilt.

1616
Shakespeare dies at age fifty-two and is buried in Stratford-upon-Avon.

1623
Thirty-six of Shakespeare's plays, collected in the famous *First Folio* edition, are published. Anne Hathaway Shakespeare dies.

1642
The Puritans close down all English theaters, which will not reopen until the Restoration of King Charles II in 1660.

1644
The Puritans demolish the Globe Theatre. A modern reconstruction opens in 1997.

Social Issues in Literature

CHAPTER 1

Background on William Shakespeare

The Life of William Shakespeare

Encyclopedia of World Biography

The Gale Encyclopedia of World Biography *provides biographical sketches of famous people that include vital statistics as well as information on the importance of the subject.* The Encyclopedia of World Biography *contains biographies of subjects as diverse as Mother Teresa, Princess Diana, Tom Clancy, and Johnnie Cochran.*

William Shakespeare is universally considered among the best writers who ever lived. His creativity and range are virtually unmatched. He was born in a rural English town but spent most of his adult career in London, writing plays for his theater company, which eventually gained enough prominence that King James I became its patron. During his more than twenty-year career, Shakespeare wrote in several genres, including histories, tragedies, comedies, and romances. Plays such as Measure for Measure *and* Antony and Cleopatra, *in particular, were notable for their exploration of sexual themes. After Shakespeare's death in 1616, two of his actors collected many of the plays into the famous* First Folio, *thus ensuring the endurance of Shakespeare's work.*

The English playwright, poet, and actor William Shakespeare (1564–1616) is generally acknowledged to be the greatest of English writers and one of the most extraordinary creators in human history.

The most crucial fact about William Shakespeare's career is that he was a popular dramatist. Born six years after Queen Elizabeth I had ascended the throne, contemporary with the

"Shakespeare, William (1564–1616)," *Encyclopedia of World Biography*, 1998. From, *Encyclopedia of World Biography*, 2E. © 2010 Cengage Learning.

high period of the English Renaissance, Shakespeare had the good luck to find in the theater of London a medium just coming into its own and an audience, drawn from a wide range of social classes, eager to reward talents of the sort he possessed. His entire life was committed to the public theater, and he seems to have written nondramatic poetry only when enforced closings of the theater made writing plays impractical. It is equally remarkable that his days in the theater were almost exactly contemporary with the theater's other outstanding achievements—the work, for example, of [fellow playwrights] Christopher Marlowe, Ben Jonson, and John Webster.

Shakespeare's Youth

Shakespeare was born on or just before April 23, 1564, in the small but then important Warwickshire town of Stratford. His mother, born Mary Arden, was the daughter of a landowner from a neighboring village. His father, John, son of a farmer, was a glove maker and trader in farm produce; he had achieved a position of some eminence in the prosperous market town by the time of his son's birth, holding a number of responsible positions in Stratford's government and serving as mayor in 1569. By 1576, however, John Shakespeare had begun to encounter the financial difficulties which were to plague him until his death in 1601.

Though no personal documents survive from Shakespeare's school years, his literary work shows the mark of the excellent if grueling education offered at the Stratford grammar school (some reminiscences of Stratford school days may have lent amusing touches to scenes in [his comedy] *The Merry Wives of Windsor*). Like other Elizabethan schoolboys, Shakespeare studied Latin grammar during the early years, then progressed to the study of logic, rhetoric, composition, oration, versification, and the monuments of Roman literature. The work was conducted in Latin and relied heavily on rote memorization and the master's rod. A plausible tradition holds that William had to discontinue his education when about 13 in order to help his father. At 18 he married Anne Hathaway, a Stratford girl. They had three children (Susanna, 1583–1649; Hamnet, 1585–1596; and his twin, Judith, 1585–1662).... Shakespeare remained actively involved in Stratford affairs throughout his life, even when living in London, and retired there at the end of his career.

The years between 1585 and 1592, having left no evidence as to Shakespeare's activities, have been the focus of considerable speculation; among other things, conjecture would have him a traveling actor or a country schoolmaster. The earliest surviving notice of his career in London is a jealous attack on the "upstart crow" by Robert Greene, a playwright, professional man of letters, and profligate [immoral person] whose career was at an end in 1592 though he was only 6 years older than Shakespeare. Greene's outcry testifies, both in its passion and in the work it implies Shakespeare had been doing for some time, that the young poet had already established himself in the capital. So does the quality of Shakespeare's first plays: It is hard to believe that even Shakespeare could have shown such mastery without several years of apprenticeship.

Early Career

Shakespeare's first extant play is probably *The Comedy of Errors* (1590; like most dates for the plays, this is conjectural and may be a year or two off), a brilliant and intricate farce involving two sets of identical twins and based on two already-complicated comedies by the Roman [writer] Plautus. Though less fully achieved, his next comedy, *The Two Gentlemen of Verona* (1591), is more prophetic of Shakespeare's later comedy, for its plot depends on such devices as a faithful girl who educates her fickle lover, romantic woods, a girl dressed as a boy, sudden reformations, music, and happy marriages at the end. The last of the first comedies, *Love's Labour's Lost* (1593), is romantic again, dealing with the attempt of three young men to withdraw from the world and women for 3 years to study in their king's "little Academe," and their quick surrender to a group of young ladies who come to lodge nearby. If the first of the comedies is most notable for its plotting and the second for its romantic elements, the third is distinguished by its dazzling language and its gallery of comic types. Already Shakespeare had learned to fuse conventional characters with convincing representations of the human life he knew.

Though little read and performed now, Shakespeare's first plays in the popular "chronicle," or history, genre are equally ambitious and impressive. Dealing with the tumultuous events of English history between the death of [King] Henry V in 1422 and the accession of Henry VII in 1485 (which began the period of Tudor stability maintained by Shakespeare's own queen), the three "parts" of *Henry VI* (1592) and *Richard III* (1594) are no tentative experiments in the form, rather they constitute a gigantic tetralogy [four-part work], in which each part is a superb play individually and an integral part of an epic sequence. Nothing so ambitious had ever been attempted in England in a form hitherto marked by slapdash formlessness.

Shakespeare's first tragedy, *Titus Andronicus* (1593), reveals similar ambition. Though its chamber of horrors—including mutilations and ingenious murders—strikes the modern reader as belonging to a theatrical tradition no longer viable, the play is in fact a brilliant and successful attempt to outdo the efforts of Shakespeare's predecessors in the lurid tradition of the revenge play.

When the theaters were closed because of plague during much of 1593–1594, Shakespeare looked to nondramatic poetry for his support and wrote two narrative masterpieces, the seriocomic *Venus and Adonis* and the tragic *The Rape of Lucrece*, for a wealthy patron, the Earl of Southampton. Both poems carry the sophisticated techniques of Elizabethan narrative verse to their highest point, drawing on the resources of Renaissance mythological and symbolic traditions.

Shakespeare's most famous poems, probably composed in this period but not published until 1609, and then not by the author, are the 154 sonnets, the supreme English examples of the form. Writing at the end of a brief, frenzied vogue for sequences of sonnets, Shakespeare found in the conventional 14-line lyric with its fixed rhyme scheme a vehicle for inexhaustible technical innovations—for Shakespeare even more than for other poets, the restrictive nature of the sonnet generates a paradoxical freedom of invention that is the life of the form—and for the expression of emotions and ideas ranging from the frivolous to the tragic. Though often suggestive of autobiographical revelation, the sonnets cannot be proved to be any the less fictions than the plays. The identity of their dedicatee, "Mr. W.H.," remains a mystery, as does the question of whether there were real-life counterparts to the famous "dark lady" and the unfaithful friend who are the subject of a number of the poems. But the chief value of these poems is intrinsic: The sonnets alone would have established Shakespeare's preeminence among English poets.

The Lord Chamberlain's Men

By 1594 Shakespeare was fully engaged in his career. In that year, he became principal writer for the successful Lord Chamberlain's Men—one of the two leading companies of actors; a regular actor in the company; and a "sharer," or partner, in the group of artist-managers who ran the entire operation and were in 1599 to have the Globe Theatre built on the south bank of the Thames. The company performed regularly in unroofed but elaborate theaters. Required by law to be set outside the city limits, these theaters were the pride of London, among the first places shown to visiting foreigners, and seated up to 3,000 people. The actors played on a huge platform stage equipped with additional playing levels and surrounded on three sides by the audience; the absence of scenery made possible a flow of scenes comparable to that of the movies, and music, costumes, and ingenious stage machinery created successful illusions under the afternoon sun.

For this company Shakespeare produced a steady outpouring of plays. The comedies include *The Taming of the Shrew* (1594), fascinating in light of the first comedies since it combines with an Italian-style plot, in which all the action occurs in one day, a more characteristically English and Shakespearean plot, the taming of Kate, in which much more time passes; *A Midsummer Night's Dream* (1595), in which "rude mechanicals," artisans without imagination, become entangled with fairies and magic potions in the moonlit woods to which young lovers have fled from a tyrannical adult society; *The Merchant of Venice* (1596), which contributed Shylock and Portia to the English literary tradition; *Much Ado About Nothing* (1598), with a melodramatic main plot whose heroine is maligned and almost driven to death by a conniving villain and a comic subplot whose Beatrice and Benedick remain the archetypical sparring lovers; *The Merry Wives of Windsor* (1599), held by tradition to have been written in response to the queen's request that Shakespeare write another play about Falstaff (who had appeared in *Henry IV*), this time in love; and in 1600 the pastoral *As You Like It*, a mature return to the woods and conventions of *The Two Gentlemen of Verona* and *A Midsummer Night's Dream*, and *Twelfth Night*, perhaps the most perfect of the comedies, a romance of identical twins separated at sea, young love, and the antics of Malvolio and Sir Toby Belch.

Shakespeare's only tragedies of the period are among his most familiar plays: *Romeo and Juliet* (1596), *Julius Caesar* (1599), and *Hamlet* (1601). Different from one another as they are, these three plays share some notable features: the setting of intense personal tragedy in a large world vividly populated by what seems like the whole range of humanity; a refusal, shared by most of Shakespeare's contemporaries in the theater, to separate comic situations and techniques from tragic; the constant presence of politics; and—a personal rather than a conventional phenomenon—a tragic structure in which what is best in the protagonist is what does him in when he finds himself in conflict with the world.

Continuing his interest in the chronicle [history play], Shakespeare wrote *King John* (1596), despite its one strong character a relatively weak play; and the second and greater tetralogy, ranging from *Richard II* (1595), in which the forceful [Henry] Bolingbroke, with an ambiguous justice on his side, deposes the weak but poetic king, through the two parts of *Henry IV* (1597), in which the wonderfully amoral, fat knight Falstaff accompanies Prince Hal, Bolingbroke's son, to *Henry V* (1599), in which Hal, who becomes king, leads a newly unified England, its civil wars temporarily at an end but sadly deprived of [comic character and friend] Falstaff and the dissident lowlife who provided so much joy in the earlier plays, to triumph over France. More impressively than the first tetralogy, the second turns history into art. Spanning the poles of comedy and tragedy, alive with a magnificent variety of unforgettable characters, linked to one another as one great play while each is a complete and independent success in its own right—the four plays pose disturbing and unanswerable questions about politics, making one ponder the frequent difference between the man capable of ruling and the man worthy of doing so, the meaning of legitimacy in office, the value of order and stability as against the value of revolutionary change, and the relation of private to public life. The plays are exuberant works of art, but they are not optimistic about man as a political animal, and their unblinkered recognition of the dynamics of history has made them increasingly popular and relevant in our own tormented era.

Three plays at the end of Elizabeth's reign are often grouped as Shakespeare's "problem plays," though no definition of that term is able successfully to differentiate them as an exclusive group. *All's Well That Ends Well* (1602) is a romantic comedy with qualities that seem bitter to many critics; like other plays of the period, by Shakespeare and by his contemporaries, it presents sexual relations between men and women in a harsh light. *Troilus and Cressida* (1602), hardest of the plays to classify generically, is a brilliant, sardonic, and disillusioned piece on the Trojan War, unusually philosophical in its language and reminiscent in some ways of *Hamlet*. The tragicomic *Measure for Measure* (1604) focuses more on sexual problems than any other play in the canon; Angelo, the puritanical and repressed man of ice who succumbs to violent sexual urges the moment he is put in temporary authority over Vienna during the duke's absence, and Isabella, the victim of his lust, are two of the most interesting characters in Shakespeare, and the bawdy city in which the action occurs suggests a London on which a new mood of modern urban hopelessness is settling.

The King's Men

Promptly upon his accession [to the English throne] in 1603, King James I, more ardently attracted to theatrical art than his predecessor, bestowed his patronage upon the Lord Chamberlain's Men, so that the flag of the King's Men now flew over the Globe [Theatre]. During his last decade in the theater, Shakespeare was to write fewer but perhaps even finer plays. Almost all the greatest tragedies belong to this period. Though they share the qualities of the earlier tragedies, taken as a group they manifest new tendencies. The heroes are dominated by passions that make their moral status increasingly ambiguous, their freedom increasingly circumscribed; similarly the society, even the cosmos, against which they strive suggests less than ever that all can ever be right in the world. As before, what destroys the hero is what is best about him.... The late tragedies are each in its own way dramas of alien-

William Shakespeare, born 1564, is considered one of the greatest playwrights and poets of all time. He wrote or collaborated with others on 38 plays and more. © Bettmann/Corbis.

ation, and their focus, like that of the histories, continues to be felt as intensely relevant to the concerns of modern men.

Othello (1604) is concerned, like other plays of the period, with sexual impurity, with the difference that that impurity is the fantasy of the protagonist about his faithful wife. Iago, the villain who drives Othello to doubt and murder, is the culmination of two distinct traditions, the "Machiavellian" conniver who uses deceit in order to subvert the order of the polity, and the Vice, a schizophrenically tragicomic devil figure from the morality plays going out of fashion as Shakespeare grew up. *King Lear* (1605), to many Shakespeare's masterpiece, is an agonizing tragic version of a comic play (itself based on mythical early English history), in which an aged king who foolishly deprives his only loving daughter of her heritage in order to leave all to her hypocritical and vicious sisters is hounded to death by a malevolent alliance which at times seems to include nature itself. Transformed from its fairy-tale-like origins, the play involves its characters and audience alike in metaphysical questions that are felt rather than thought.

Macbeth (1606), similarly based on English chronicle material, concentrates on the problems of evil and freedom, convincingly mingles the supernatural with a representation of history, and makes a paradoxically sympathetic hero of a murderer who sins against family and state—a man in some respects worse than the villain of *Hamlet*.

Dramatizing stories from [Roman author] Plutarch's [book] *Parallel Lives, Antony and Cleopatra* and *Coriolanus* (both written in 1607–1608) embody Shakespeare's bitterest images of political life, the former by setting against the call to Roman duty the temptation to liberating sexual passion, the latter by pitting a protagonist who cannot live with hypocrisy against a society built on it. Both of these tragedies present ancient history with a vividness that makes it seem contemporary, though the sensuousness of *Antony and Cleopatra*, the richness of its detail, the ebullience of its language, and the seductive character of its heroine have made it far more popular than the harsh and austere *Coriolanus*. One more tragedy, *Timon of Athens*, similarly based on Plutarch, was written during this period, though its date is obscure. Despite its abundant brilliance, few find it a fully satisfactory play, and some critics have speculated that what we have may be an incomplete draft. The handful of tragedies that Shakespeare wrote between 1604 and 1608 comprises an astonishing series of worlds different from one another, ... some of the most complex and vivid characters in all the plays, and a variety of new structural techniques.

Last Plays and Death

A final group of plays takes a turn in a new direction. Commonly called the "romances," *Pericles[, Prince of Tyre]* (1607), *Cymbeline* (1609), *The Winter's Tale* (1611), and *The Tempest* (1611) share their conventions with the tragicomedy that had been growing popular since the early years of the century. Particularly they resemble in some respects plays written by [Francis] Beaumont and [John] Fletcher for the private theatrical company whose operation the King's Men took over in 1608. While such work in the hands of others, however, tended to reflect the socially and intellectually narrow interests of an elite audience, Shakespeare turned the fashionable mode into a new kind of personal art form. Though less searing than the great tragedies, these plays have a unique power to move and are in the realm of the highest art. *Pericles* and *Cymbeline* seem somewhat tentative and experimental, though both are superb plays. *The Winter's Tale*, however, is one of Shakespeare's best plays. Like a rewriting of *Othello* in its first acts, it turns miraculously into pastoral comedy in its last. *The Tempest* is the most popular and perhaps the finest of the group. Prospero, shipwrecked on an island and dominating it with magic which he renounces at the end, may well be intended as an image of Shakespeare himself; in any event, the play is like a retrospective glance over the plays of the two previous decades.

After the composition of *The Tempest*, which many regard as an explicit farewell to art, Shakespeare retired to Stratford, returning to London to compose *Henry VIII* and *The Two Noble Kinsmen* in 1613; neither of these plays seems to have fired his imagination. In 1616, at the age of 52, he was dead. His reputation grew quickly, and his work has continued to seem to each generation like its own most precious discovery. His value to his own age is suggested by the fact that two fellow actors performed the virtually unprecedented act in 1623 of gathering his plays together and publishing them in the folio edition. Without their efforts, since Shakespeare was apparently not interested in publication, many of the plays would not have survived.

Shakespeare Was Knowledgeable About Sex

Stanley Wells

Stanley Wells is an English Shakespearean scholar. He has served as director of the Shakespeare Institute at the University of Birmingham, England. His books include Shakespeare: For All Time, Shakespeare & Co. *and* Shakespeare: The Poet and His Plays.

Wells poses the question what did Shakespeare know about sex? From Shakespeare's writings, particularly the 154 sonnets, Wells then attempts to answer this question, extrapolating from the poems to the life. Wells maintains that the poems are more personal than Shakespeare's plays, which are deliberate fictions. The sonnets, Wells writes, tell us more about the man. They hint at Shakespeare's extramarital affairs and strongly suggest that he might have contracted a sexually transmitted disease at some point. Despite his supposed extramarital dalliances, Shakespeare was not involved in any known sex scandals, Wells writes, but both of his daughters were.

What do we know, or what may we legitimately infer, about Shakespeare's own knowledge and experience of sex? The closeness of family life in his boyhood, along with the normal experiences of puberty, including gossip and, probably, furtive fumblings at school and elsewhere, would no doubt have informed his early sexual knowledge. Some of the literature that he read at grammar school would have been at least mildly erotic, some of it homoerotic. It has been said, for instance, that his reading there

---

Stanley Wells, *Shakespeare, Sex, & Love*, 2010, pp. 69–82. Copyright © 2010 by Oxford University Press. All rights reserved. Reproduced by permission.

would have encompassed erotic verse by poets like Horace and Virgil, who wooed both genders. To have mastered classical Latin was to have received a reasonably candid sexual education from poets who were unabashedly libertine and bisexual. It is a fact that an English schoolboy in Shakespeare's day would have learned far more about homosexuality from his classroom reading than a student in the age of [American sex researcher of the 1940s and 1950s Alfred] Kinsey.

A Quick Learner

Shakespeare seems to have proceeded with exceptional speed from theory to practice, at least in heterosexuality. Between 1570 and 1630 the average age for first marriage among men in Stratford, calculated on the basis of 106 known cases, was between twenty and thirty, with the 'greatest number of marriages (fifteen) taking place when the bridegroom was twenty-four'. In itself this may seem an arid statistic, but to anyone interested in Shakespeare it springs to dramatic life when we learn that he was one of only three men in the town over the sixty-year period to be recorded as having married before he was twenty years old, and the only one whose bride was pregnant at the time. So early a marriage must suggest that he was an early developer sexually, especially since he lived at a time when the onset of puberty is generally believed to have been later than it is now. It may also count as negative evidence in the much-debated question of whether he was apprenticed to his father, or indeed to anyone else, as glover or butcher or whatever. Laws were and are often broken, but the fact remains that it was against the law for apprentices to be married. (Is it even thinkable that Shakespeare got Anne pregnant so that he had to marry and therefore could avoid being apprenticed?!)

The evidence I have given about prosecutions for prenuptial fornication shows that Shakespeare was lucky to escape punishment for getting Anne Hathaway pregnant before marriage. We can only conjecture whether there was any special reason for his good fortune, such as his father's prominent position in the town's hierarchy. Desire to minimize scandal may also help to explain why the marriage did not take place in Stratford itself—it is not recorded in the parish registers, which are full for this period. Where exactly it did is a matter for conjecture; the neighbouring villages of Temple Grafton and Luddington are among those often suggested, but there is no hard evidence. The Shakespeares' first daughter, Susanna, was born on 26 May 1583, within six months of the marriage.... Twins, Hamnet and Judith, followed about 21 months later—they were baptized on 2 February 1585, a normal time span allowing for the fact that conception within the period of lactation is unusual. There were no more children....

Many Temptations

Shakespeare must often have been absent from home in pursuit of his profession, and temptation must often have been put in his way. As we have seen, stories about assignations between actors and members of their audience were rife. The best known of all such stories concerns Shakespeare himself:

> Upon a time when [Richard] Burbage played Richard the Third there was a citizen grew so far in liking with him, that before she went from the play she appointed him to come that night unto her by the name of Richard the Third. Shakespeare, overhearing their conclusion, went before, was entertained and at his game ere Burbage came. Then, message being brought that Richard the Third was at the door, Shakespeare caused return to be made that William the Conqueror was before Richard the Third.

That is an entry dated 13 March 1602 in the notebook kept by the lawyer John Manningham, of the Middle Temple, which also contains the first recorded performance of *Twelfth Night*, in the same year. His joke was repeated, in different form, in the eighteenth century, in Thomas Wilkes's *A General View of the Stage* (1759). Wilkes cannot have got it from Manningham, whose diary remained unpublished until the nineteenth century. But the existence of two different versions of the same anecdote does not prove that it was true, only that it was thought to be a good enough story to be worth repeating.

There are also hints that boy actors held attractions for men as well as women. For instance [English Puritan writer] John Rainolds, in his *Th'Overthrow of Stage Plays* (1599), asks 'what sparkles of lust to that vice the putting of women's attire on men may kindle in unclean affections, as [Roman emperor] Nero showed in Sporus [young Roman boy], [reputedly bisexual Roman emperor] Heliogabalus in himself; yea certain, who grew not to such excess of impudency [shamelessness], yet arguing the same in causing their boys to wear long hair like women.' Undeniably the appearance of men, especially of the aristocracy, in relation to clothes as well as to length of hair resembled that of women. [Shakespeare's patron] the Earl of Southampton was proud of his long swathes of hair, which is conspicuous in a portrait painted around the time that Shakespeare dedicated poems to him. But it does not necessarily denote effeminacy. . . .

Shakespeare and Sexually Transmitted Disease

The implication of sexual laxity in Manningham's anecdote relates to a theory, propounded with particular force by two women biographers, Katherine Duncan-Jones and Germaine Greer, that a venereal disease, such as syphilis, may have been a direct or contributory cause of Shakespeare's death. Images of venereal disease appear especially in relation to [Shakespeare's comic character] Falstaff in a relatively lighthearted manner in the tavern scenes of *Henry IV* parts 1 and 2 and, probably by coincidence, become more frequent and more graphic in plays written in the four or five years soon following the date of Manningham's diary entry. They are most common in [the plays] *Measure for Measure, Troilus and Cressida, Pericles[, Prince of Tyre], King Lear*, and *Timon of Athens*. There are also possible allusions in the two last-printed sonnets, which include references to

> ... a seething bath which yet men prove
>
> Against strange maladies a sovereign cure.
>
> But at my mistress' eyes love's brand new fired,
>
> The boy [Cupid] for trial needs would touch my breast.
>
> I, sick withal, the help of bath desired,
>
> And thither hied, a sad distempered guest,
>
> But found no cure; the bath for my help lies
>
> Where Cupid got new fire: my mistress' eyes.

There are at least two strong arguments against supposing that the allusions in the plays along with the sonnets imply that the author himself suffered from the diseases he writes about. One is, quite simply, that writers do not need to have personal experience of their subject matter. Shakespeare does not need to have been a rapist to have written [his poem] *The Rape of Lucrece*, or a murderer to have written [the tragedy] *Macbeth*. As for the sonnets, the final two in particular are, of all the poems in the collection, the ones with the clearest literary sources. Both go back to a Greek epigram in which

> Love slept, having put his torch in the care of the nymphs; but the nymphs said to one another 'Why wait? Would that together with this we could quench the fire in the hearts of men'. But the torch set fire even to the water and with hot water thenceforth the Love-Nymphs fill the bath.

Shakespeare's 'bath' is sometimes interpreted as a reference to the city of Bath, with its healing waters. It is true that hot mercury baths were used to treat syphilis, but 'editors who have imagined the poet setting off with his diseases to Bath to take the waters [ignore] the fact that sweating tubs must have been available in London'. If any of the sonnets are, as is often claimed, 'literary exercises', and therefore useless as biography, these highly derivative poems are they. . . .

Sex and the Sonnets

Are there other ways in which the sonnets may inform us about Shakespeare's personal sex life? The question of whether they are directly based on his own experience, or whether they are, as is often suggested, 'literary exercises', fictitious projections of imagined experiences, is hotly debated. It is a question to which there could, perhaps, be more than one answer: this to say, some of them could be more closely related than others to his personal life. I have emphasized what I believe to be the fallacy of reading the 154 poems as a unified collection, suggesting for instance that not all of the first 126 poems are necessarily addressed to a male, and that those so addressed are not necessarily all addressed to the same male. Similarly it is possible that some of the poems are more or less genuinely personal outpourings while others are more fictional imaginings. As a dramatist, Shakespeare spent most of his life imagining himself into the lives and minds of fictitious persons. The sonnets might be as it were dramatic monologues with no basis in real life. Some of them could be straightforward exercises in lyric form.

If I must defend my personal belief, nevertheless, that some, indeed many of them, reflect circumstances of the author's own emotional and sexual life, it will be on several different grounds. One is that, while it is impossible to date the poems with any precision, there are good reasons for believing that many of them were written during the 1590s,

Circa 1950: The cover of the first edition of William Shakespeare's Sonnets, dated 1609. © Hulton Archive/Getty Images.

when the love sonnet was a fashionable form, and that their late, and possibly unauthorized publication long after this fashion had died down suggests at least that they were not written as professional exercises, to make money and to enhance the poet's reputation, as the narrative poems clearly were.

Another far more subjective reason is that to me the exploration of, especially, emotional situations of extreme anguish in some of the poems has the ring of authenticity. I should not be able to defend this position on purely intellectual grounds, since the man who could portray the emotional and sexual anguish of characters such as Troilus and Othello could have written no less convincingly of such passions in nondramatic poems. But I could point to the fact that in the only poems in which the protagonist has a name, it is Shakespeare's own—Will. This distinguishes the collection from all others of the period, in which an addressee has a personal name, usually of a romantic cast such as Fidessa, Delia, or Stella....

The Sonnets as Autobiography?

So, if we think of these poems in autobiographical terms, what do they tell us? One, they show that he was indeed, and probably frequently, unfaithful to his wife. Furthermore we need to consider the triangular relationship involving friend and mistress adumbrated both in the poems printed earlier in the collection, up to number 126, which include all those clearly addressed to a male, and in those printed later, from number 127 onwards, which include the 'dark lady' sonnets.

It has been justly remarked that, uniquely among Elizabethan sonnet collections, 'for the first time in the entire history of the sonnet, the desired object [the writer assumes a single object] is flawed'. Sonnet 35 alludes to an unnamed 'trespass', a 'sensual fault' which the poet forgives. Number 41 opens a mini-sequence with what starts as a mild enough admission that it is understandable that the friend's youth and beauty should cause a woman to woo him:

And when a woman woos, what woman's son

Will sourly leave her till he have prevailed?

But in the sestet [the last six lines of a sonnet] the poet more bitterly expresses dismay that the woman with whom the friend is linked is the poet's own mistress:

> Ay me, but yet thou mightst my seat forbear,
>
> And chide thy beauty and thy straying youth
>
> Who lead thee in their riot even there
>
> Where thou art forced to break a two-fold troth:
>
> Hers, by thy beauty tempting her to thee,
>
> Thine, by thy beauty being false to me.

Then the next poem says that, though the poet dearly loved the woman, 'That she hath thee is of my wailing chief, / A loss in love that touches me more nearly.' Other poems, too, such as sonnets 93, 95–6, and 120, show a troubled sense of a friend's transgressions.

The same theme emerges in the 'dark lady' poems. Sonnet 133 curses 'that heart that makes my heart to groan / For that deep wound it gives my friend and me.' Nothing is left. The woman has both betrayed the poet and enslaved his 'sweet'st friend', his 'next self', so that 'Of him, myself, and thee I am forsaken.' Sonnet 134 runs straight on to beg the 'covetous' woman to restore his 'kind' friend to him. But there is no hope: 'Him have I lost; thou hast both him and me; / He pays the whole, and yet am I not free.' Then, ... in sonnet 135 he puns tortuously and despairingly on the many possible senses of the word 'will' which include the name of both the poet and another man, desire, penis, and vagina. The following poem continues the wordplay, with seven uses of the word 'will', concluding categorically with 'my name is Will.'

I find it difficult not to read these poems as expressions of resentment at sexual infidelity on the part of both a male friend and a woman with whom he is linked. To me, the intensity of the poet's involvement with both one or more males and at least one woman suggests that he had both homosexual and extramarital heterosexual relationships. But there is everything to suggest that if he did so he was conscious of betraying ideals, of behaving out of unreasonable human frailty in ways that part of him deplored: his eyes 'know what beauty is, see where it lies, / Yet what the best is take the worst to be' (137); 'she that makes me sin / Awards me pain' (141); 'Love is my sin' and his mistress's lips 'have sealed false bonds of love as oft as mine, / Robbed others' beds' revenues of their rents' (142); 'Past cure I am, now reason is past care, / And frantic mad with evermore unrest' (147); 'In loving thee thou know'st I am forsworn . . . But why of two oaths' breach do I accuse thee / When I break twenty?' (152). He is, he acknowledges, the victim of lust which overwhelms reason:

> The'expense of spirit in a waste of shame
>
> Is lust in action; and till action, lust
>
> Is perjured, murd'rous, bloody, full of blame,
>
> Savage, extreme, rude, cruel, not to trust,
>
> Enjoyed no sooner but despisèd straight,
>
> Past reason hunted, and no sooner had
>
> Past reason hated as a swallowed bait
>
> On purpose laid to make the taker mad;
>
> Mad in pursuit and in possession so,
>
> Had, having, and in quest to have, extreme;
>
> A bliss in proof and proved, a very woe;
>
> Before, a joy proposed; behind, a dream.
>
> All this the world well knows, yet none knows well

> To shun the heaven that leads men to this
> hell. (Sonnet 129)

This is a man with a conscience, betrayed by the turbulent sexuality that—if Shakespeare really is speaking of himself—led to his early marriage....

Shakespeare and Sex Scandals

We have no documentary evidence deriving from legal sources of Shakespeare himself being involved, whether innocently or not, in sexual scandals. The same is true of his wife Anne. Domestically, the family stuck together. Shakespeare lived in several sets of lodgings in London, but there is nothing to show that he occupied them with anyone else. Or that he did not. There is no evidence of where the family lived in Stratford during the early years of marriage. It is usually assumed that they shared the family home with Shakespeare's parents, though Germaine Greer conjectures that they may have had a separate household before the purchase of the rather grand establishment, New Place, in 1597, fifteen years after they married. If so, there is no trace of it in the records. From 1597 until they married, their daughters Judith and Susanna presumably lived in New Place with their mother, and with their father whenever he came back to Stratford.

The sonnets appeared in print in 1609. The facts that they bear a dedication signed with the initials of the publisher, Thomas Thorpe, and that there is reason to believe that Shakespeare did not proofread the volume suggest that although the book was entered in the normal way in the Stationers' Register [a record book], on 20 May, the publication was unauthorized. Unlike the narrative poems, it seems to have been a publishing failure. The actor Edward Alleyn bought a copy in June, soon after it appeared. But it did not go into a second edition, which suggests that, although the publisher seems to have regarded its appearance as something of a coup—'Shakespeare's sonnets, never before imprinted', reads the title page—it flopped. Some scholars think that the book may have been suppressed, possibly on moral grounds, but this is mere conjecture. Others have supposed that, though Shakespeare may have wanted it to be published, he may have waited until after his mother died (she was buried on 9 September 1608) so as not to embarrass her. But his wife and daughters were still alive. Whether the publication of this apparent sequence of intimate revelations affected them, or the family's reputation, we simply do not know. Conceivably the revelation of marital infidelity through the publication of these poems affected his daughters' reputation: towards the end of his life both of them were involved in sexual scandals, though they appear to have been victims rather than offenders. Susanna was the subject of gossip which she was brave enough to challenge publicly. In July 1613 she sued one John Lane for slander in the Consistory Court at Worcester on the grounds that he had reported that she 'had the running of the reins'—that is, a venereal infection—'and had been naught'—committed adultery—'with Ralph Smith', a Stratford hat maker. Her accuser, presumably unable to substantiate his charge, failed to turn up, and was excommunicated. (This is the subject of Peter Whelan's 1998 play, *The Herbal Bed*.) At the time of the accusation the Halls [Susanna and her husband, John] were living in New Place, no doubt with Anne and William, who by this time had virtually given up his literary career and was presumably spending more time at home.

In addition, scandal marred the marriage of Shakespeare's younger daughter, Judith, though it was not directly detrimental to her personal reputation. On 10 February 1616, at the age of 31, she married Thomas Quiney, a vintner and member of a prominent Stratford family. His father, Richard, was a neighbour of Shakespeare and wrote the only surviving letter addressed to him. Judith, like her mother and father before her, married in haste, failing to obtain the special licence required because it was Lent. As a result she and her husband were excommunicated. The reason for the haste must be related to the fact that the bridegroom had been carrying on an affair with another woman, Margaret Wheeler. On 15 March she and a child to whom she had given birth, presumably conceived by Quiney, were buried in Stratford. On 26 March, only six weeks after he married, he was brought to trial for incontinence with Margaret, and 'confessed that he had had carnal intercourse' with her. The vicar who had married him sentenced him to perform public penance 'clothed in a sheet (according to custom) for three Sundays' in Holy Trinity Church. In the event he was let down lightly; having offered five shillings to the poor of the town, he was required merely 'to acknowledge his fault in his own attire before the Minister of Bishopton [close to Stratford] . . . and to certify this at the next court'.

Shortly before all this happened, probably in January, Shakespeare had drafted a will which shows great concern for family values. It apportions his money and property mainly between his two daughters, though also with bequests to other family members and to friends. His elder daughter, Susanna, and her husband, John Hall, are the main beneficiaries, as well as being appointed his executors. On 25 March, the day before Quiney appeared in court, Shakespeare made changes which suggest that in the light of what had happened, he was anxious to ring-fence Judith's interests. His bequests to her are substantial: £100 as a marriage portion and £50 more on condition that she surrender to Susanna her rights in a cottage on Chapel Lane, a silver-gilt bowl, and the interest on another £150 which would go to her or, if she had died, to her children three years after the date of the will; but she would receive this only as long as she was married, and her husband could claim it only if he settled lands of equal value on her. In the event, and despite its inauspicious start, her marriage was long-lasting and she had three children, all of whom died young. The eldest, baptized, like her sister's child, only nine months after she married, had the given name of Shakespeare, as if in tribute to his grandfather.

The Impossibility of Really Knowing

In writing of Shakespeare's sex life, I have not attempted to draw evidence from his plays. It is clear from these that he had a deep understanding of sexual desire and of romantic love, of bodily rapture, and of sexual nausea: that he could imagine himself into the minds and imaginations of accepted and rejected lovers, that he had so vivid a sense of the torments inflicted by sexual jealousy that it would be easy, especially in the light of parallels with the sonnets, to suspect more or less direct projections of his personal life in characters such as Othello and Leontes [king in *The Winter's Tale*].... Shakespeare presents his dramas as fictions, and most of them derive partly from preexisting literary and other sources. These are transformed by his imagination, which of course was fed by experience, but, as with the sonnets, it is ultimately impossible to sift the imagined from the real.

Social Issues in Literature

CHAPTER 2

Sexuality in *A Midsummer Night's Dream*

A Midsummer Night's Dream Is a War Between the Sexes

Ace G. Pilkington and Olga A. Pilkington

Ace G. Pilkington is a professor of English and history at Dixie State College and literary seminar director at the Utah Shakespeare Festival. He has published more than one hundred poems, articles, reviews, and short stories. Olga A. Pilkington has published articles in Russia and the United States. The Pilkingtons wrote the filmography for Michael Flachmann's Shakespeare from Page to Stage.

The authors characterize A Midsummer Night's Dream *as a series of battles between its male and female characters. The play revolves around the power struggles of men and women. The women in the play challenge patriarchal society by defying the men who try to control their behavior. Throughout the play, Shakespeare references older folk beliefs that have strong elements of feminine freedom and power. The old folk stories are connected to present with comparisons of the Amazon goddess to Queen Elizabeth, a woman who managed to wield power in a patriarchal society.*

A *Midsummer Night's Dream* is a play about women defying men. It is also, of course, about many other things, but, nevertheless, this play contains a series of stories where women defy men at almost every level from the marital to the martial, from recalcitrant brides to warring Amazons. For example, Theseus and Hippolyta meet on the battlefield, and their relationship continues to have its conflicts. Oberon and Titania nearly come to blows over her fixation on the change-

---

Ace G. Pilkington and Olga A. Pilkington, "Folktales, Myths, and Amazons in A Midsummer Night's Dream," *Insights*, 2005. Copyright © 2005 by Ace and Olga Pilkington. All rights reserved. Reproduced by permission.

ling child, a mania that Oberon cannot break directly—even with all his magic—but only by replacing one of Titania's obsessions with another. Hermia refuses to obey her father—or Theseus, come to that. Helena will not accept Demetrius's rejection of her, chasing him down (like another Helena in *All's Well That Ends Well*) while she points out that, as a woman, she should not be chasing him at all (particularly in the woods at night). And because this is Shakespeare and comedy, not one of these assertive, argumentative, occasionally armor-bearing females comes to a bad end as a result of her aggression.

Midsummer Games

Shakespeare set the stage for these battles of the sexes by invoking the old and (by the lights of the Protestant Reformation) destabilizing fertility rituals of midsummer. As Stephen Greenblatt says, "These folk customs, all firmly rooted in the Midlands, had a significant impact upon Shakespeare's imagination, fashioning his sense of the theater even more than the morality plays. . . . Folk culture is everywhere in his work, in the web of allusions and in the underlying structures. The lovers who meet in the Athenian woods in *A Midsummer Night's Dream* are reminiscent of May Day lovers" (Stephen Greenblatt, *Will in the World: How Shakespeare Became Shakespeare* [New York: W.W. Norton & Company, 2004], 40). It is not too much to say that midsummer festivals are about fertility and also about older systems of belief, pagan gods, and less patriarchal social structures. In the words of Harold F. Brooks, "It was in the May game that the tradition of the ancient fertility cult lived on. The 'observaunce to May' was 'everybody's pastime': it was at least as much a popular custom as a courtly one. There is a correspondence in the dream's whole action with the movement of the May game, from the town to the woods and back, bringing home the summer" (Harold F. Brooks ed., *The Arden Edition of the Works of Will-*

Circa 1565, The Queen of England, Elizabeth I (1533–1603). © Topical Press Agency/Hulton Royals Collection/Getty Images.

iam Shakespeare: A Midsummer Night's Dream [London: Methuen, 1983], lxix). There were such games with their half-forgotten, half-numinous rituals scattered all over Europe. Some of them are especially pertinent to Shakespeare's story. Sir James Frazer found, for example, "that in Sweden the ceremonies associated elsewhere with May Day or Whitsuntide commonly take place at Midsummer." He also wrote (in 1922) that in "the Swedish province of Blekinge they still choose a Midsummer's Bride" who "selects for herself a Bridegroom" (Sir James George Frazer, *The Golden Bough* [New York: The Macmillan Company, 1940], 133). Frazer tells of Briancon (Dauphine) where "on May Day the lads wrap up in green leaves a young fellow whose sweetheart has deserted him.... He lies down on the ground and feigns to be asleep. Then a girl who likes him, and would marry him, comes and wakes him and raising him up offers him her arm" (Frazer, 133).

Religion and Folk Memories

Often, the new religion (or the latest version of the new religion as was the case in Elizabethan England) connects such ceremonies and their older gods to the dead and to evil as a way of suppressing them, but folk memories are long, and the stories have within themselves the seeds of their own resurrection. Katharine Briggs points out such forms of suppression and the "close connection" between ghosts, fairies, White Ladies, "the Irish 'Bean Fionn,'" and Guenevere in the Arthurian cycle" (Katharine Briggs, *A Dictionary of Fairies* [Harmondsworth, Middlesex: Penguin, 1977], 430). The rusalka offers an especially clear example of the process. The rusalka survives in Slavic folklore as a water spirit, fertility spirit, fairy, nymph, ghost, or sometimes all of the above. "Weaving flowers into her hair, she was the very picture of eroticism." Like the supernatural creatures in *A Midsummer Night's Dream*, "in early summer . . . the rusalki would leave their homes in the rivers and streams to dance together in the woods and fields (*Forests of the Vampire: Slavic Myth* [New York: Barnes and Noble, 2003], 66–67). "The rusalka's description shows very handily the inversion which occurs to an important pre-Christian figure with the growing influence of Christianity. What was once sacred becomes profane; what was positive becomes negative.

The rusalka is probably a descendant of Mokosh, the goddess of fertility, bounty, and moisture, and the protectress of women's work and the fate of maidens. Her taming by the cross may reflect just that—the taming of belief in the rusalka as a powerful supernatural figure due to the influence of Christianity" (Philippa Rappaport, "If It Dries Out, It's No Good: Women, Hair and Rusalki Beliefs," *SEEFA Journal*, vol. 4, no. 1, Spring 1999: 55-64).

Folklore and Feminine Freedom

It is likely that the rusalka is a remnant of an older society in which women were freer to express their sexuality and to disagree with men. The folk beliefs which Shakespeare is invoking also have a strong element of feminine freedom about them. Brides may choose their husbands, goddesses grant fertility and survival, and women succeed as warriors. Interestingly enough in view of his miniaturization of some of his fairies, Shakespeare has worked hard to restore others to their full divine power. Titania is not merely Queen of the Fairies; she is also Diana/Artemis, in the words of Sir James George Frazer, a goddess of "wild beasts, a mistress of woods and hills, of lonely glades and sounding rivers.... Diana ... may be described as a goddess of nature in general and of fertility in particular." As a goddess of fertility, "it behooved Diana to have a male partner." Folk beliefs have her coupled with "the priest who bore the title of King of the Wood." Frazer suggests that "the aim of their union would be to promote the fruitfulness of the earth, of animals, and of mankind" (Frazer, 140–141) all of which is threatened, should "Titania cross her Oberon" (Shakespeare, *A Midsummer Night's Dream*, Wolfgang Clemen ed. [New York: Signet, 1963], 2.1 19). But, of course, the situation in *A Midsummer Night's Dream* of bad weather to be corrected by the sympathetic magic of a male-female union is exactly what the folk rituals were.

Titania as Diana/Artemis is also an Amazon goddess; a deity who is, as the Amazons were thought to be, both virginal and sexual. Titania's obligations as such a goddess would be with "fairy grace" (4.1 402) to bless the marriage of Theseus and his warrior bride. Hippolyta and Theseus's way to the altar lay through the path of war. Amazons and Hippolyta as their queen are part of the pre-Christian society where "women hold religious power" and thus possess more freedoms. As Lyn Webster Wilde says, "The Amazons ... are borderline beings ...: they are women with the power of women but they express that power in a masculine way" (Lyn Webster Wilde, *On the Trail of the Women Warriors* [New York: St. Martin's Press, 2000], 105). In *A Midsummer Night's Dream*,

Shakespeare has given us an Amazon goddess, an Amazon Queen, and for good measure, Queen Elizabeth, who was sometimes viewed as an Amazon.

"During her lifetime, Queen Elizabeth was identified with several Amazonian personages, including Diana" (Gail Kern Paster and Skiles Howard, eds., *William Shakespeare A Midsummer Night's Dream: Texts and Contexts* [New York: Bedford/St. Martin's, 1999], 199). So, in the end, in that all-inclusive way of his, Shakespeare took his audience into the mythic past, only to bring them again to their present, where a new myth was being built, and a new woman wielded power.

A *Midsummer Night's Dream* Urges Brides to the Wedding Bed

David Wiles

David Wiles is a professor of theater at the University of London. His books include Theatre and Citizenship: The History of a Practice; Shakespeare's Clown: Actor and Text in the Elizabethan Playhouse; *and* Mask and Performance in Greek Tragedy: From Ancient Festival to Modern Experimentation.

Wiles places A Midsummer Night's Dream *firmly in the tradition of the epithalamium, a poem written expressly for newly married women on their way to the wedding bed. The form was popular among writers and Shakespearean contemporaries such as Edmund Spenser, John Donne, and Ben Jonson. A* Midsummer Night's Dream, *Wiles suggests, shares many of the attributes of the poems of such writers. Shakespeare also uses the mock relationship between Nick Bottom and Titania as a parody of what a true marriage should be, though Wiles believes that their relationship is consummated in the flowery bower. The result of such carnal acts is offspring, and Wiles writes that once the sexual act between Bottom and Titania is concluded, Oberon obtains from Titania what every husband of the day most prized—a male offspring.*

The closing speeches of *A Midsummer Night's Dream* constitute the kind of finale that we would expect to find at the end of a wedding masque [a form of aristocratic entertainment including music and dance]. No other play by Shakespeare ends quite like it. *Love's Labour's Lost* and *The*

David Wiles, *Shakespeare's Almanac: A Midsummer Night's Dream, Marriage, and the Elizabethan Calendar*, 1993, pp. 114–125. Copyright © 1993 by Boydell & Brewer. All rights reserved. Reproduced by permission.

Tempest celebrate a betrothal, not a wedding. In *As You Like It*, the appearance of Hymen [god of marriage] in a kind of masque suggests that the couples should be understood as married rather than betrothed at the end of the play, but the moment of marriage is left vague. Orthodox ceremonial does not seem to belong in the Forest of Arden [setting of *As You Like It*]. The formality of the ending is the formality of a conventional theatrical finale, with four couples gathered on stage for a celebratory dance. Unlike these three plays, *A Midsummer Night's Dream* displays a complete lack of concern with the process of courtship. The rites of courtship—a first encounter in a romantic environment, the interchanging of love tokens, the composing of love verses—are all completed before the action of the play begins. The play is concerned with the actual physical union of male and female. . . .

A Poem for the Marriage Bed

The finale of Shakespeare's play has all the attributes of an epithalamium [marriage poem]. In act 4 we see a reveille, followed by a procession to the church. Unlike [poets Edmund] Spenser and [John] Donne, Shakespeare omits the actual ceremony in the 'temple'. He does stage the wedding masque (in a grotesque inverted form), and he represents the departure of the bridal couples to bed. The events within the bedchamber, transposed and burlesqued, are represented through the encounter of [Nick] Bottom and Titania. At the end of Shakespeare's play it is after midnight, the new day is waxing, and it is time for the consummation. Theseus and Hippolyta, Hermia and Lysander, Helena and Demetrius have all left and are supposed in bed. Puck evokes the noises and spirits of the night that Spenser warned of in his *Epithalamion*:

> Ne let the Pouke, nor other evil sprites,
>
> Ne let mischievous witches with their charms,

Ne let Hobgoblins, names whose sense we see not,

Fray us with things that be not.

Let not the screech-owl, nor the stork be heard:

Nor the night raven that still deadly yells

Nor damnèd ghosts called up with mighty spells.

When Shakespeare's Puck appears with his cleansing broom, he evokes the same 'screech-owl', the same 'sprites' arisen like ghosts from gaping graves. Unlike Spenser's Puck, Shakespeare's Puck alias 'Hobgoblin' (II.i.40) and his demonic companions cease to threaten and become instead protectors of the marriage bed....

A Sexuality-Charged Scene

Within the body of Shakespeare's play, Titania's bower is an obvious symbol of the marriage bed. We have seen how Spenser merges the concepts of the 'bridal bower and genial bed' by virtue of the herbs and flowers placed inside the bedchamber. [English poet George] Wither in his 'Epithalamion' of 1613 rouses the bride in the morning because the 'Bride-Chamber lies to dressing'. [English dramatist Ben] Jonson in [his wedding masque] *Hymenaei* speaks of 'the nuptial-room' as 'the chaste bower, which Cypria strows / With many a lilly, many a rose'. In 'Lord Hay's Masque' [written by Thomas Campion], roses are plucked from Flora's bower and strewn about the stage, and the masquers all pass into the bower after they have removed their green garments of chastity. It is easy to see the link between bed and bower when we recall that Elizabethan beds were surrounded by curtains. In performance, whether in the public playhouse or in a private dining hall, Titania would most likely have led Bottom behind a curtain. By extension, a 'bower' commonly becomes a metaphor for the enclosing body of the woman, and we have seen how this idea is exploited in 'Lord Hay's Masque'.

The encounter between Bottom and Titania can be seen as an inversion or burlesque of the real consummation that will occur after the play is over. Like the secluded marriage bed blessed by holy water, Titania's bower is described as 'consecrated' (III.ii.7).... Titania confidently promises Bottom sexual satisfaction in her bower when she promises to purge his mortal grossness, and to have pearls fetched from the deep. In a double entendre, she tells her fairies to escort Bottom 'to bed, and to arise'. Bottom's escort of male fairies can be equated with the bridegroom-men whose role would be to lead the groom to the bedchamber. The four fairies are instructed to dance and to feast Bottom before lighting him to bed. Their duty is to ensure that he does not have 'sleeping eyes' (III.i.166), but is sexually aroused. The names of the fairies suggest sexual attributes. Bottom's attention passes from Cobweb—used to staunch bleeding—to Peaseblossom—a flower which will grow into a phallic peascod—and finally to Mustardseed—the tiny potent seed which grows into a huge tree. When [critic] Jan Kott interprets Peaseblossom, Mustardseed, Cobweb and Moth as ingredients for an aphrodisiac, he misses only the element of parody, for these are folk remedies for common complaints. We might recall the electuaries which [English poet Geoffrey] Chaucer's January [in 'The Merchant's Tale' in *Canterbury Tales*] took in a vain attempt to make himself capable of a bridegroom's duties. Bottom, like January, is the antithesis of the model bridegroom.

When the pair finally re-emerge from the bower, consummation must be deemed to have taken place. Many productions have succeeded in eliminating this possibility by conflating the offstage bower with the onstage flowery bank, and so keeping the couple safely in view. The text lends no support to this chaste interpretation. Bottom's garland of roses plucked from the bower symbolizes his sexual conquest. Titania still has appetite for more, but Bottom only wants to sleep. Sexually exhausted, he seeks a filled honey-bag. Titania offers him 'new nuts'. Sensing that it is morning, and time to shave ('I am marvellous hairy about the face'), he accepts the offer of breakfast, with rough music to accompany the reveille. The details owe not a little to 'The Merchant's Tale', where Chaucer refers to the bristly chin of January in the wedding bed, to his breakfasting and singing in the morning before he falls asleep, to his 'coltish' behaviour, and grotesque appearance with nightcap and lean, sagging neck.

Bottom and Titania's Relationship as a Parody Marriage

The encounter between Bottom and Titania is a parodic inversion. A real bride should be modest, not sexually voracious, a virgin and not sexually experienced. The real groom should display more sexual enthusiasm, yet not surrender to animal instinct. Jonson is clear about the man's duty:

> Tonight is Venus' vigil kept.
>
> This night no bridegroom ever slept;
>
> And if the fair bride do,
>
> The married say 'tis his fault too.

Bottom's failure to stay awake is conceived as the ultimate form of inappropriate behaviour in a nuptial context. In the context of a real wedding, we can see how the parody would have a social function of some importance. The night is to be an initiation for both parties, and is a rite of passage that has no modern equivalent. A couple who have only met each other a few times in relatively formal circumstances are suddenly going to meet naked under the sheets, with an obligation to give a good account of themselves the next morning.

The shyness and distress of the bride is a stock motif in epithalamia. Spenser urges:

> Let no lamenting cries, nor doleful tears,
>
> Be heard all night within nor yet without.

Jonson in *Hymenaei* pictures a 'faint and trembling bride' on her sacrificial altar, and he urges the thirteen-year-old girl:

> Shrink not, soft virgin, you will love
>
> Anon what you so fear to prove.

For [poet Robert] Herrick the bride is afraid of the physical experience which lies ahead, and the groom must be persistent:

> O Venus! thou, to whom is known
>
> The best way how to loose the zone
>
> Of virgins! Tell the maid,
>
> She need not be afraid:
>
> And bid the youth apply
>
> Close kisses, if she cry:
>
> And charge, he not forebears
>
> Her, though she woo with tears.

Herrick suggests that the bridesmaids are also likely to be weeping, faced with the loss of youth and companionship. He associates the grief of the bridesmaids with a festive cycle which, as we saw in the last chapter, is linked to rites of passage. A girl goes out with a partner in May, but if she has not secured a husband by Midsummer Eve, she tries at that point to foretell who she will be paired with in the coming spring.

> Virgins, weep not; 'twill come, when,
>
> As she, so you'll be ripe for men.
>
> Then grieve her not, with saying
>
> She must no more a-Maying:

Or by Rose-buds divine

Who'll be her Valentine.

While Titania is the antithesis of the shrinking bride in *A Midsummer Night's Dream*, Hermia is the embodiment. She denies Lysander 'bed-room' and insists that they behave as 'Becomes a virtuous bachelor and a maid' (II.ii.58). Her subsequent Freudian [relating to the psychoanalytic theories of Sigmund Freud] dream of a snake demonstrates her fear of sexuality. Her maidenly modesty, combined with a desire to sleep, results in her losing the love of Lysander. In the peculiar context of a wedding night, Hermia's behaviour becomes no more acceptable than that of Titania. A real bride is required to perform a dialectical miracle, and find an intermediate mode of behaviour that avoids both evils: modesty and lust.

Followers of Venus

Once the sexual act has taken place in Titania's bower, Oberon is able to obtain from Titania that which he most wants, the boy. Titania's withholding of the boy is the source of all the dissent in Fairyland, and the chaotic inversion of the seasons. Pregnancy is vividly and rapturously evoked, likened to the way a sail grows 'big-bellied with the wanton wind' (II.i.129). Titania is custodian of the boy, but after her consummation with Bottom, she transfers the boy to Oberon's bower. The symbolism is clear in an epithalamic context. The boy sought by Oberon parallels the male heir which all bridegrooms seek from their brides. The poets are explicit on this subject. Spenser hopes that Cynthia, who has charge of 'women's labours' may 'the chaste womb inform with timely seed'. Genius is asked to ensure that the 'timely fruit of this same night' arrives safely. Jonson calls for 'the birth, by Cynthia hasted' in the epithalamium to *Hymenaei*, and in the epithalamium after the 'Haddington Masque' he calls for a babe who will 'Wear the long honours of his father's deed'. The masculine pronoun seemed self-evident. Herrick echoes the theme, and we notice how dew is again associated with procreation:

May the bed, and this short night,

Know the fullness of delight!

Pleasures, many here attend ye,

And ere long, a boy, Love send ye,

Curled and comely, and so trim,

Maids (in time) may ravish him.

Thus a dew of graces fall

On ye both; goodnight to all.

Aristocratic marriages were undertaken in order that a family line could be continued. Brides were under enormous psychological pressure to yield up a male child. The pressure which Oberon places upon a reluctant Titania echoes that urgent social demand. The entire central action of the play is a dreamlike (or nightmare) evocation of a wedding night. The Athenian scenes are associated with the public, patriarchal aspect of marriage. The young lovers have to obtain parental consent at the start of the play, and in the last act they conform to the social expectation that males will be capable of witty banter, females will be modestly silent. The woodland scenes are associated with the private, nocturnal, female-dominated aspect of marriage. The wood, closely associated with the maying ceremony, functions as an extended May/nuptial bower. As in a nuptial, it is 'deep midnight' when the lovers escape to the secrecy of the 'bower'. Here they fall prey to Puck and other malicious spirits. The long-delayed sexual act is suggested mimetically [by mimicry or imitation] by the dance when Oberon and Titania hold hands and 'rock the ground whereon these sleepers be' (IV.i.85). In the morning when the lovers are woken to the rough music of the hounds, they receive a humiliating reveille. The reveille, as we have seen, was a time when the newly married couple had to give an account of themselves, and satisfy interrogators that intercourse had taken place. As in the dream, so in reality a hunting song was often used to awaken the newlyweds. What the lovers in the play have learned from their experience is not clear, but in the extra-theatrical world of the audience, an actual bridal couple may well have done their share of learning and adjusting. It was not only [Titania] who found the conflict between Venus [goddess of love] and Diana [goddess of chastity] very hard to reconcile. Every young bride was expected on her wedding night to put aside the cult of chastity and in an instant become a votary [devoted follower] of Venus.

The Ass Motif in *The Comedy of Errors* and *A Midsummer Night's Dream*

Deborah Baker Wyrick

Deborah Baker Wyrick is an associate professor of English at North Carolina State University. She is the author of Jonathan Swift and the Vested Word, *and she has published articles on various seventeenth- and eighteenth-century minor writers.*

Wyrick writes that Shakespeare uses Nick Bottom's transformation in A Midsummer Night's Dream, *where he is given the head of an ass, as a multifaceted metaphor. However perversely or innocently one wants to read the scene between Bottom and Titania, Wyrick suggests, there is certainly a sexual component to the scene, a "beauty and the beast" motif that serves as a metaphor for a young woman's mastering her fear of sexuality. Bottom and Titania's liaison becomes a comic filter for the real-life romances of the four Athenian lovers wandering through the forest at night. Bottom's hybrid nature allows Shakespeare to represent a key duality in the play: the conflict between order—in the archetypal Apollonian sense—and sexuality and disorder—represented by the god Dionysius.*

One of the most ubiquitous epithets in Shakespearean drama is "ass." Since it carries the primary significance of an ignorant fellow, a perverse fool, or a conceited dolt, the word can be counted upon to stimulate audience laughter.[1] The frequency of its appearance in Shakespeare's plays, however, makes one suspect that it is a word rich in thematic as-

---

Deborah Baker Wyrick, "The Ass Motif in *The Comedy of Errors* and *A Midsummer Night's Dream*," *Shakespeare Quarterly*, vol. 33, no. 4, Winter 1982, pp. 432–448. Copyright © 1982 by Johns Hopkins University Press. All rights reserved. Reproduced by permission.

sociations and in dramatic applications.² Far from functioning merely as a simple synonym for a stupid blunderer, the word "ass"—whether used as a simile, as a metaphor, or as a pun—has a protean ability to convey economically a number of connotations. These connotations arise causally from the speaker, from the situation, and from the larger verbal context in which the word operates. In similar fashion, the effects of the word radiate outward, sometimes revealing aspects of the speaker or of the person spoken to, sometimes focusing a parodic subplot, sometimes amplifying a theme. Although "ass" is sprinkled throughout the Shakespearean canon, it is most prevalent in the early comedies, especially in *The Comedy of Errors* and *A Midsummer Night's Dream*. An examination of the ass motif's appearance in these plays can illuminate Shakespeare's inventive transformation of this seemingly unassuming word into a complex verbal cipher.

I

Before turning to the specific Shakespearean texts, it is necessary to explore background material pertaining to the symbolic associations of the ass. For example, biblical asses are generally benign, even exemplary; they are the progenitors of the "admirable ass" tradition. The most memorable ass in the Old Testament is Balaam's articulate animal (Numbers xxii). This ass was not only granted a sight of the angel of the Lord; she was also designated a communicatory channel for God. Her vision prevented her from following Balaam's commands, aroused her master's anger, which translated itself into unjustified blows, and precipitated divine reproach and Balaam's ultimate redemption from sin. Thus, Balaam's ass represents wisdom rather than stupidity. The story also conveys the idea of the ass as a victim of physical abuse, as a symbol of suffering—an interpretation darkened in the account of the ass's ignominious end in Jeremiah xxii.19.

The picture of an ass patiently bearing savage mistreatment as well as its occupational burdens leads to the image of the animal as a type of Christ, one reinforced by Christ's choice of the lowly ass as a vehicle for his triumphal entry into Jerusalem (see Matthew xxi.5; prefigured in Zechariah ix.9). Christ, then, is the cosmic ass, patiently and humbly bearing the world's burden of sin. A more tenuous identification between Christ and the ass is found in reports by Plutarch and Tacitus asserting that the Jews adored the ass because it discovered springs of water in the desert during the exodus; the ass, therefore, is also a type of Christ as the wellspring of life. Perhaps this tradition provoked the underground convention, mentioned by Tertullian and Cecilius Felix, of portraying Christ with an ass's head.[3]

In contrast to the implied identification of the ass with Christ, the Bible also sets forth the equivalence of the ass with the fool. The third verse of Proverbs xxvi, the chapter about fools and folly, states: "A whip for the horse, a bridle for the ass, and a rod for the fool's back." Not only are fools and asses juxtaposed in a manner which leads one to infer a metaphorical connection between them, but they are linked with references to instruments of restraint and of chastisement. Thus, the ass's connotations are broadened to include folly and punishment appropriate to folly, as well as Christological patience and punishment unduly received. The ass as a type of fool was destined to overpower the ass as a type of Christ—a tradition that re-emerged only sporadically in Western thought, often in strange forms such as the eccentric homologic catechism which compared the anatomy of an ass with the architecture of a cathedral—or the ridiculously parodic Asses' Feast, a medieval institution connected with the Feast of Fools in which an ass was led through the church, an Asses' Liturgy was sung by the clergy in a harsh bray, and a merry alcoholic eucharist was celebrated by all concerned.[4]

In the Renaissance, the ass as a symbol of stupidity and as a religious allegory combined in an alternative tradition, the *asinus portans mysteria*. Whitney's emblem, *Non tibi, sed religioni*, shows worshipers venerating a statue of Isis borne on the back of an ass, the animal being an image of vanity because it thinks the crowd is lauding it rather than the goddess.[5] Nevertheless, the ass as an admirably patient, long-suffering beast—even if not specifically presented as an analogue of Christ—remained a continuing iconological undercurrent during the Middle Ages and the Renaissance.[6]

One reason for the strength of the "foolish ass" tradition was the influx of classical elements. Aesop's fables demonstrate the stupidity of asses; but more important to Shakespeare is the ass-lore in Ovid. The eleventh book of the *Metamorphoses* recounts Apollo's "gift" of ass's ears to the tone-deaf Midas, who had the temerity to prefer Pan's rude pipings to Apollo's sweet strains. In Golding's translation of Ovid, "Apollo could not suffer well his [Midas'] foolish eares too keepe / Theyr humaine shape, but drew them wyde, and made them long and deepe".[7] Midas' asinine musical judgment—one shared by his Shakespearean counterpart, Bottom—evoked an emblematic transformation. This confluence of stupidity, bad taste in music, and asininity parallels the Greek proverbial question used by Boethius, as translated by Chaucer: "Artow like an asse to the harpe?"[8] Boethius subsequently expands his identification of asshood to include general laziness, and he glosses this type of metamorphosis as an outward and visible sign of inward and spiritual vice: "Yf he be slow, and astonyd, and lache, he lyveth as an ass.... 'O feble and light is the hand of Circes the enchauntresse, that chaungeth the bodyes of folk into beestes, to regard and to comparysoun of mutacioun that is makid by vices!'"[9] In the Renaissance, this theme is echoed in Whitney's emblem, *Homines voluptatibus transformantur*, which reads in part: "Some had the shape of ... Asses ... Which showes those foolishe sorte, whome wicked love doth thrall ... and have no sense at all ... Oh stoppe your eares, and shutte your eies, of Circes cuppe beware".[10] The idea of an ass as the embodiment of foolishness is given more direct expression by Cesare Ripa and Piero Valeriano; their emblems of Obstinacy and Ignorance show figures holding or porting asses' heads.[11]

In the sixteenth century, the ass was not merely an allegory of stupidity, but was also connected specifically with the fool proper. Asses' ears wagged as a conventionalized feature of the fool's hood.[12] Similarly, Erasmus' Folie distributes asses' ears to fools and dissemblers. For example, Chaloner's 1549 translation of *Moriae Encomium* states:

> So that not so muche as they can dissemble me [Dame Folie], who take vpon their most semblant of wysedome, and walke lyke Asses in Lyons skynne. That althoughe they counterfeite what they can, yet on some syde their longe eares pearyng foorth, dooe discouer them to come to Midas progenie.... Suche men therfore, that in deede are archdoltes, and woulde be taken yet for sages and philosophers, maie I not aptelie calle theim foolelosophers?[13]

Nevertheless, Erasmus conflates fools and asses in ways not solely derogatory. He also praises the humility and holiness of the Natural Fool, who is "nearest to the bluntness of brute beastes, and attempts nothyng beyonde mans degree" (p. 48). This variety of fool is loved by Christ, who "delited much in theyr *simplicitee,* euin lyke as those kindes of dumme beastes were most acceptable vnto hym, that were fardest remoued from all Foxelike wylinesse. And therefore chose he rathest to ryde on an asse ..." (p. 117). By the end of the book, Christ himself is identified as this sort of holy fool.

It is, however, the "foolelosophers" rather than the sanctified asses who dominate the iconography of the period. Woodcuts spotlighting fools in ass-eared hoods decorate Barclay's 1509 translation of Brant's *Das Narrenschiff,* furthermore, these illustrations frequently show the fool in close proximity with the ass. The textual connections between fools and asses range from the emblematic ("assys erys for our folys a lyuray is,") to moral commentaries ("To infernall Fenn doth this pore Asse oppresse / And to an asse moste lyke he is doutless") and obscene narratives:[14]

> Under the Asse tayle thoughe it be no thynge pure
>
> Yet many seke and grope for the vyle fatnes
>
> Gatherynge togyther the fowle dunge and ordure
>
> Such as they that for treasour and ryches
>
> Whyle they ar yonge in theyre chefe lustynes
>
> An agyd woman taketh to theyr wyfe
>
> Lesynge theyr young, and shortynge so theyr lyfe.

This coarse congregation of asses, women, and the posterior parts leads to the last set of connotations associated with the word. Renaissance pronunciation allowed "ass" to serve as a paronomasia with "arse," a pun frequently coupled with a similar play upon the word "tail." Then as now, moreover, these words could refer directly to the genitals as well as generally to the rump.[15] Thus, in another broadly bawdy sense, the word "ass" could stand for women as bearers of sexual burdens. These associations manifested themselves memorably in medieval punishments for prostitutes; in France, for example, whores were sentenced to ride naked upon asses, head to tail.[16] Perhaps one reason for the appropriateness of the sinner's mount is the tradition of the ass as a particularly priapic animal.[17]

It is this strain of ass-lore which dictated the transformation of the erotically adventurous "hero" of Apuleius' *The Golden Ass*, a transformation which added the salacious spice of bestiality to Lucius' sexual encounters. Nevertheless, even Apuleius' "licentious ass" finally transcends his fleshly incarceration through the transforming power of love, one beautifully allegorized in the interpolated "Cupid and Psyche" episode. In the main narrative, after accepting Divine Wisdom in the guise of Isis, Lucius shifts his role to that of an actor in a different ass tradition—the *asinus portans mysteria*. In Adlington's 1566 edition of Apuleius, the high-minded interpretation of the tale is in the ascendant; the translator explains that the book is to be treated in the *Ovide moralisé* manner:

> Verily under the wrap of this transformation is taxed the life of moral men, when as we suffer our minds so as to be drowned in the sensual lusts of the flesh and the beastly pleasure thereof ... that we lose wholly the use of reason and virtue, which properly should be in a man, and play the parts of brute and savage beasts.[18]

Thus, even as a sexual cipher the ass is unstable; under his shaggy skin lurks a remarkable ability to shift symbolic significance. The "licentious ass," the "foolish ass," and the "admirable ass" inhabit one hide.

The ass is a braying oxymoron. It is self-evident that Shakespeare did not consult Proverbs, Boethius, Brant, or Adlington every time he decided to permit one of his characters to call someone an ass. It should be equally clear that Shakespeare had at his disposal a tantalizingly slippery word, the connotations of which ranged from the sacred to the scurrilous. It would have been uncharacteristic of the playwright's inventiveness had he not exploited the linguistic, thematic, and structural possibilities inherent in the word "ass."

II

Although *The Comedy of Errors* generally is considered Shakespeare's first comedy, it demonstrates one of the author's most adroit manipulations of the ass motif. Both dialectical poles of the play, one of which arises from the potentially serious framing device and the other from the knock-about central plot of mistaken identity, are contained within the ass image. The concept unites them into a comic synthesis which keeps the spectator firmly aware of the prevailing comic vision. The play's first explicit mention of the word "ass" occurs in act II, scene i, when Adriana is railing against Antipholus of Ephesus' tardiness and infidelity. Luciana, invoking traditional marital roles, attempts to restrain her sister's precipitous jealousy: "O know that he is the bridle of your will" (I. 13). Adriana, in a permutation of Proverbs xxvi.3, retorts: "[T]here's none but asses will be bridled so" (I. 14).[19] To an audience used to interpreting the epithet "ass" as an indication of foolishness, Adriana's remark immediately cues a stock response of laughter, which heightens the sense of comic distance reinforced by the artificially patterned rhyming couplets of the dialogue.

But Adriana's implied ass simile is not limited to equating wives with fools. Whereas Luciana's subsequent speech refers to physical abuse ("Why, headstrong liberty is lashed with woe," I. 15), a reward of the disobedient ass, Adriana twists the idea of master and beast of burden into a complaint about wives' sexual slavery to husbands (II. 26, 34–36). Luciana keeps counseling patience, also playing on the word "bear" ("Till he come home again, I could forbear," I. 31). The interchange is interrupted by Dromio of Ephesus' news of the strange behavior of the man he supposes to be his master and his account of the beatings received at his hands—beatings which Adriana threatens to continue (II.i.78).[20] The audience has just witnessed the encounter between Antipholus of Syracuse and Dromio of Ephesus in the previous scene; now the physical abuse and the pregnant wording (e.g., Dromio of Ephesus: "Perchance you will not bear them patiently," I.ii.86) present in the earlier scene take on added significance after having been filtered through the specific mention of "ass." On one level, Shakespeare's use of "ass" in act II, scene i urges the audience to maintain its emotional distance; on another, it distinguishes the rash and sexually troubled character of Adriana from the patient and sexually innocent character of Luciana; on a third, it helps establish the theme of patience, the virtue which will finally permit the comic resolution; on a fourth, it retroactively identifies Dromio of Ephesus with the long-suffering ass tradition and prepares for the comic metamorphosis of both Dromios into asses—a change which underscores the entire situational and imagistic core of the play, the illusion-producing qualities of mistaken identity.

The second scene of the first act, the first scene of the second act, and the second scene of the second act form a triptych picturing the initial mistaking of Antipholus of Syracuse. Its central panel, the one containing the play's first mention of the word "ass," casts a symbolic shadow back upon the preceding panel, the one in which Dromio of Ephesus is treated like an ass. Correspondingly, the third panel presents Dromio of Syracuse beaten like a foolish beast of burden (II.ii.22–52). When the Syracusan Dromio and Antipholus encounter Adriana and Luciana in the first great comic crisis of mistaken identity, all four characters express their wonder about the effects of the metamorphic atmosphere which seems to be pervading their lives (Adriana: "I am not Adriana, nor thy wife," l. 111; Antipholus of Syracuse: "In Ephesus I am but two hours old, / As strange unto your town as to your talk," ll. 147–48; Luciana: "how the world is changed with you," l. 151; Dromio of Syracuse: "This is the fairy land," l. 188).[21] At the end of the scene, these confused musings reach a crescendo centered around the familiar image of the ass:

Dromio S.:

I am transformed, master, am I not?

Antipholus S.:

I think thou art, in mind, and so am I.

Dromio S.:

> Nay master, both in mind and in my shape.
> Antipholus S.:
> Thou hast thine own form.
> Dromio S.:
> No, I am an ape.
> Luciana.:
> If thou art changed to aught, 'tis to an ass.
> Dromio S.:
> 'Tis true; she rides me, and I long for grass.
> 'Tis so, I am an ass; else it could never be
> But I should know her as well as she knows me.
> Adriana:
> Come, come, no longer will I be a fool.
> (II.ii.194–203)

The immediate effect of this passage is to mitigate the mood of malignant metamorphosis. The stichomythia, the jingling couplets, and the bawdy suggestiveness inherent in Dromio of Syracuse's definition of his own asininity reestablish the comic spirit and reassure the audience that these transformations are risible and reversible. Furthermore, since the "she" refers to Luciana, Dromio's remark may prefigure Antipholus of Syracuse's infatuation; certainly, the tone of the slave's discourse provides a perfect anticipatory burlesque of his master's Petrarchan hyberbole—a rhapsody which does, however, contain similar sorts of sexual double entendres (III.i.29–51; see particularly the last four lines).

Dromio of Syracuse's flippant self-assessment also serves to differentiate him from his twin brother. The Syracusan slave presents himself as a Lylyan servant, saucy and ribald. His asininity springs from both the "foolish ass" and the "licentious ass" traditions. In contrast, Dromio of Ephesus is an "admirable ass"—a patient sufferer bearing unwarranted punishment. Shakespeare emphasizes the comparison by scene juxtaposition. Act III, scene i—the first panel of the second

triptych, one which presents the initial mistaking of Antipholus of Ephesus—immediately takes up the ass motif:
Antipholus E.:
I think thou art an ass.
Dromio E.:
Marry, so it doth appear
By the wrongs I suffer and the blows I bear.
I should kick, being kicked; and, being at that pass,
You could keep it from my heels and beware of an ass.
(III.i.14–18)

Although both the stock response of laughter conjured up by the word "ass" and the odd four-beat but syllabically jammed couplets in which Dromio of Ephesus speaks brush a comic veneer over this interchange, the slave is not presented solely as a figure of mirth. Instead, like Balaam's animal, he is abused for trying to act in his irascible master's best interests. Shakespeare's intent to make comparable metamorphic but contrastable emblematic asses of the Dromios is further underscored when the Ephesian servant yells through the door to his brother: "If thou hadst been Dromio to-day in my place, / Thou wouldst have changed thy face for a name, or thy name for an ass" (ll. 46–47). Concurrently, the Ephesian Dromio's forbearing patience plays against his master's headstrong nature, setting the stage for Antipholus of Ephesus' rage when he later is barred from his own house.

"Ass" as a mediating metaphor bridges the two wooing scenes in act III, scene ii. After Dromio of Syracuse asks whether his master knows him, Antipholus of Syracuse replies, "Thou art Dromio, thou art my man, thou art thyself" (III.ii.76–77), only to be answered, "I am an ass, I am a woman's man, and besides myself" (ll. 78–79). This structurally parallel interchange brings Antipholus of Syracuse from the ethereal cosmology with which he praises his love for Luciana ("My sole earth's heaven, and my heaven's claim," l. 64) to a bantering participation in the mundane geography which depicts Dromio of Syracuse's run-in with Luce ("she is spherical, like a globe; I could find out countries in her," ll. 114–15). It also reaffirms the farcical bawdiness which marks the Dromios and reestablishes the metamorphic theme and its attendant Circean animal imagery (e.g., Dromio of Syracuse: "She had transformed me to a curtal dog, and made me turn i' the wheel," ll. 144–45; Antipholus of Syracuse: "There's none but witches do inhabit here," l. 154).[22] The scene ends as Angelo enters bearing the chain which brings about the comic catastrophe of Antipholus of Ephesus, who is hauled off to prison for nonpayment of debts in act IV, scene i, the last panel of the triptych figuring the destruction of his public reputation.

The final triptych finds all participants wandering deeper and deeper in illusions. The seeming metamorphoses are complete. Adriana's impatience has reached its zenith and has allowed her mentally to transform her husband into a hideous apparition (IV.iii. 17–22); Antipholus of Syracuse's fear that he is lost in a maze of sanity-annihilating sorcery has become conviction (IV.iii.37–39). Therefore, the slapstick buffeting of Dromio of Ephesus in the last panel of the triptych highlights the comic tone of the play at a point when the audience may have been tempted to forget it. Here, too, Shakespeare uses fast-paced, punning dialogue to lead up to his repetition of the word "ass," buttressing the humor in a scene replete with grim potential. Nevertheless, Dromio of Ephesus' remarkable speech about his own asininity offers a glimpse into the serious underside of comedy—the real world in which suffering is not always relieved by time's revolution, by love's reconciliation, or by order's restoration.[23] After the incensed Antipholus of Ephesus says, "Thou art sensible in nothing but blows, / And so is an ass" (IV.iv.25–26), Dromio of Ephesus replies:

> I am an ass indeed; you may prove it by my long ears. I have served him from the hour of my nativity to this instant, and have nothing at his hands for my service but blows. When I am cold, he heats me with beating; when I

am warm, he cools me with beating. I am waked with it when I sleep, raised with it when I sit, driven out of doors with it when I go from home, welcomed home with it when I return; nay, I bear it on my shoulders, as a beggar wont her brat; and, I think, when he hath lamed me, I shall beg with it from door to door. (IV.iv.27–36)

The Ecclesiastical cadence of the speech, as well as its sententious message, momentarily bestows upon Dromio of Ephesus a mantle of Christological humility and suffering. To be sure, this passage is neither long nor strong enough to permit one to view *The Comedy of Errors* as a religious allegory acted out by a troupe of Elizabethan vaudevillians; but it does invest the action with some of the tonal texture that characterizes the finest Shakespearean comedy and helps make this play more than a cleverly constructed set piece.

Before an audience can really begin to interpret the action as a sort of *Divina Commedia*, the ridiculous Dr. Pinch exorcises the metamorphic demons and engages other characters in silly swashbuckling. The comic perspective is firm once again; the stage is set for the happy resolution.

This resolution not only clears up the mistaken identities of the Antipholi and the Dromios; it also brings to a close the frame story of Egeon and Aemilia. Shakespeare does not make explicit use of the ass motif in V.i, just as he had not in I.i. Nevertheless, the web of associations he has woven around the word "ass" in the play's tripartite central portion extends to the flanking scenes. The idea of long-suffering patience, symbolized by the burden-bearing ass "marked" by blows, is applied to Egeon by the Duke in I.i.140–41: "Hapless Egeon, whom the fates have marked / To bear the extremity of dire mishap!" Since this language resembles that used by Dromio of Ephesus in I.ii.82–86, one can assume that Egeon and the Ephesian Dromio are connected thematically and act as antitheses to rash and abusive characters like Adriana and Antipholus of Ephesus. In the last scene of the comedy, the virtue of patience has prevailed, as Egeon is reabsorbed into his family and as Dromio of Ephesus is allowed the play's final harmonious words.

In addition, Adriana and Dromio of Syracuse's idea of women as metaphoric asses bearing sexual burdens is corrected in the play's first and last scenes. In I.i.46 Egeon explains that the female role in the cycle of sex and procreation is "pleasing punishment." In V.i.344 Aemilia uses a gentle pun on the word "burden" to describe the birth of her sons; in V.i.404 she maintains that the real burden is the loss of loved ones, not the bearing of a husband's sexual and social will or the begetting of children. Finally, the theme of metamorphosis which has crystalized around the servants' figurative transformations into asses is explicitly stated by the Duke. In words which recall Whitney's emblem, he says: "I think you all have drunk of Circe's cup" (V.i.271). This declaration paves the way for the playworld's release from the bonds and burdens of confused identity. The spell of Circe is replaced by the loving knowledge of Aemilia, which restores the social ties rent asunder by asinine actions and foolish mistakes.

In *The Comedy of Errors*, the ass motif has performed a variety of services. By its sheer iteration, it unifies the play; by its primary appeal to laughter, it helps establish the comic perspective at crucial points in the action; by its varying connotations, it aids in character delineation; by its metaphorical operation, it acts as a paradigm of metamorphosis. In a broad sense, all characters are asses; in their unrelenting unawareness of each other's presence in Ephesus, they form an iconographic parade of ignorance assembled from the pages of Ripa and Valeriano. Ultimately, however, the same complex of associations that informs the *asinus portans mysteria* emblem is at work in *The Comedy of Errors*. The ass may be foolish and licentious, his mis-takings making him a target of laughter, but he has been chosen to carry the reconciling promise of wisdom.

III

The ass motif is not employed in such a complex manner in the next three comedies in the canon. It is primarily used as a verbal projectile in *The Two Gentlemen of Verona* (II.iii.33; V.ii.28) and *Love's Labor's Lost* (II.i.44; V.ii.617–20). In *The Taming of the Shrew*, it functions as an extended bawdy pun (II.i.200–220). It is *A Midsummer Night's Dream*, the enchanting culmination of Shakespeare's first phase of comic development, which displays the image in its most brilliant and comic form. Bully Bottom, foolishly resplendent in a real ass's head, reigns supreme—a walking, talking, ruminating visual metaphor.[24] He represents the apotheosis of asininity. His palpably translated presence synthesizes the "admirable ass," the "foolish ass," and the "licentious ass" traditions; his unselfconsciously ludicrous appearance forms an essential component of the play's comic machinery, emblematizes his own character and talents, and comments upon the play's interconnected themes of metamorphosis, imagination, and love.

The most obvious classical analogue for Bottom's metamorphosis is Lucius' transformation in Apuleius' *The Golden Ass*. Both "heroes" are given asinine characteristics by supernatural agencies. Furthermore, Apuleius' "Cupid and Psyche" story—in which Venus uses Cupid to make Psyche fall in love with a vile thing—is paralleled by one plot strand in *A Midsummer Night's Dream*—in which Oberon uses Puck to make Titania fall in love with a vile thing.[25] Neither plan works out as expected. Psyche becomes enamored with Cupid, and Titania's ethereal advances appear to be lost on the down-to-earth Bottom.[26] Nevertheless, an undercurrent of sexuality pulsates throughout the midsummer night "affair." Even if one does not accept the Fairy Queen's loving transport as a debasing education in the subject of phallic dimensions and procreative fantasies or as a cruel descent into the "dark sphere of animal love-making,"[27] the Titania-Bottom episode seems to partake of the "Beauty and the Beast" archetype—a mythic

Titania awakening, 1785-1790, by Johann Heinrich Fussli (1741-1825), oil on canvas. © DEA PICTURE LIBRARY/De Agostini/Getty Images.

pattern which subconsciously serves as a means of mastering sexual fear.[28] This interpretation adds to the sense of sexual uneasiness which does surface occasionally throughout the play in forms including Theseus' threats to Hermia of involuntary celibacy (I.i.65–78), Oberon and Titania's extra-marital liaisons (II.i.64–80), Hermia's refusal to lie near her love (II.ii.53–61), and Helena's lack of feminine self-confidence (ll.ii.94–95). In addition, Bottom acts as a punishment for Titania's transgression against natural sexual cycles—her unwillingness to allow the changeling boy to leave the childhood zone of female influence and enter the adolescent zone of masculine influence. Bottom, for all his rustic practicality in the face of supernatural events, represents—at least in part— the "licentious ass" tradition.

Subliminal erotic perversity notwithstanding, the audience's predominant response to the dalliance between the ass and the Fairy Queen is one of amusement. In a general sense, it is comedy of the grotesque—a theatrical translation of the essentially dramatic and humorous tension found in medieval cathedrals where gargoyles crouch near saints and angels.[29] Since this order of comedy is built on strong antitheses, the overall juxtaposition of the dainty sprite and the "palpable gross" monster creates a comically incongruous spectacle embellished with equally incongruous flourishes—the homely song, the orders to the fairy attendants, the flowery garland decking the ass's nose. Shakespeare produces a double antithesis, however, by switching the expected attributes of the characters: Titania exhibits the amorous aggressiveness one would anticipate from a lusty beast; Bottom reacts with the reserve one would anticipate from a virtuous lady. In this manner, Shakespeare captures the audience's emotions by staging a comic tableau which carries with it set expectations, and he immediately releases these emotions by reversing the roles of the tableau's central figures—thereby allowing the audience to enjoy the ridiculous scenes from a safe distance. Thus, the episode—carefully placed in the middle of the play, divided in order to flank the central love confusion of the noble youths—functions as a comic filter through which the nocturnal adventures of the Athenian quartet should be viewed. In this playworld, love's metamorphoses are comic, not malevolent; Titania and Bottom's release from the spell of Cupid's flower prefigures the awakening of the four lovers into the daylight world of festive comic resolution.

In a more specific sense, the humor of the Titania-Bottom interlude arises from the ass's head proper. The word "ass" provoked a stock response of laughter and a host of connotations such as ignorance, folly, and doltishness. And if the word itself could elicit a chuckle, the apparition would produce guffaws. On an Elizabethan stage, Bottom would appear as an emblem incarnate, an actualized epithet. If Shakespeare had merely wanted to display a hybrid monster, he could have followed the Theseus legend by creating a Minotaurian Bottom complete with bull's head;[30] if he had merely wanted to present a picture of licentiousness, he could have given Bottom the attributes of a goat or an ape. The playwright must have had the "foolish ass" tradition in mind when he chose the animal with which to conflate Bottom.

Like Erasmus and Brant, Shakespeare uses the ass emblem to exemplify mankind's folly.[31] Bottom's metamorphosis, which begins with a rustic carol and ends with a reference to tongs and bones, would also remind a playgoer of Ovid and Lyly's accounts of the musically unfortunate Midas, "first a golden foole, now a leaden ass."[32] More important, perhaps, is the appropriateness of the transformation to Bottom's personality. Throughout *A Midsummer Night's Dream*, he is a fool. His unhesitatingly literal approach to dramatic art and magical illusion demolishes the fragile fabrics of both.[33] His malapropisms mark a verbal consanguinity with Dogberry, another famous Shakespearean ass; both characters join the brotherhood of those unable to interpret the facts of their situations and oblivious to truths about themselves. Therefore, Bottom's ass's head—in a comic rendition of the more frightening Circean pattern—is a physical translation of a spirtual reality.

Yet Bottom does not come across as a simple foolish bumpkin. He is never a figure of derision—except, perhaps, to the playworld's Athenian audience, whose supercilious and punning jeers at his dramatic performance (V.i.151–52, 300–304) engender from the real world's audience a response sympathetic to the weaver. Bottom's enthusiasm, good humor, and indefatigable theatrical esprit not only command affection but also inspire a sort of respect.[34]

Particularly when he utters his "Bottom's Dream" soliloquy, he becomes an "admirable ass." His scrambled scripture and inarticulate wonder link him with Erasmus' sacred natural fool. Like Balaam's ass, Bottom appears as a divinely inspired oracle, "the anointed innocent singled out for a kind of grace not despite but because of his doltishness."[35] When Bottom falteringly exclaims that "[t]he eye of man hath not heard, the ear of man hath not seen, man's hand is not able to taste, his tongue to conceive nor his heart to report what my dream was" (IV.i.208–11), he erects a comically impenetrable synaesthetic barrier against asinine exegesis. In the process, he is able to partake in "the bottome of Goddes secretes" referred to at the end of the Pauline passage which he so wisely and foolishly garbles.[36] In a spontaneously humble act of negative mysticism, he removes the "I" from the "I-Thou" equation by stating that "[i]t shall be called 'Bottom's Dream,' because it hath no bottom" (IV.i.212–13) and by recognizing his rightful role as a mouthpiece for—not as a focus of—mystery. Like Dromio of Ephesus' resonant speech on patient suffering, Bottom's account of his "most rare vision" (IV.i.203) briefly irradiates a comically human ass with an aureole of sanctity. He becomes an *asinus portans mysteria*.

This comically profound moment remains but a moment—a metaphysical flash that flares and expires before it can be apprehended. The references to play-acting framing Bottom's recounting of his dream keep the vision from seeping through the seams of the comic structure and flooding the play with theological significance. As was the case in *The Comedy of Errors*, religious associations contribute to the texture of *A Midsummer Night's Dream* without determining the play's formative pattern. The major themes of the play—love, metamorphosis, and art—do not have to be explained in theological terms. They do, however, intersect in the figure of the translated Bottom.

Bottom's connection with the themes of *A Midsummer Night's Dream* is not particularly subtle. But, of course, neither is the figure of Bottom in the ass's head. In general, his amatory interlude with Titania acts as the comic axis around which spin the love affairs of the other societal orders represented in the play—the giddy infatuations of the Athenian youths, the quarrel and reconciliation of the Fairy King and Queen, the order-establishing marriage of Theseus and Hippolyta, and the burlesque coda of "Pyramus and Thisbe" which Bottom himself helps present. Bottom's parts in the play-within-the-play and in the set piece with Titania form a ridiculous extreme of humorous literal-mindedness to balance the extreme of enraptured illusion which motivates the intoxicated lovers.[37] The fact that as Titania's *amoroso* he is actually an ass and that as Pyramus he is called an ass reinforces the Shakespearean warning that love sees "not with the eyes, but with the mind, / And therefore is winged Cupid painted blind" (I.i.234–35). Titania's discovery of beauty in Bottom's hirsute head thus comically echoes the chameleon affections of Lysander and Demetrius as they perceive first Hermia, then Helena, as paragons of pulchritude. Love-madness turns men and women into Cupid's fools. It is left to the play's most patently "foolish ass" to draw the moral from the situation, that "reason and love keep little company together nowadays" (III.i.130–31).

Among other things, Bottom's ass's head is a blatantly literal rendition of the theme of metamorphosis which permeates the play. *A Midsummer Night's Dream* is in essence Ovidian, set in a moon-drenched metamorphic woodland inhabited by shape-shifting, illusion-knitting agents and subjects.[38] Bottom is the tangible symbol of this metamorphic mist. As he tries to act all parts, to speak in all voices, Bottom casts himself as a seeker after metamorphosis.[39] Like the gold-hungry Midas, the transformation-hungry weaver gets his wish. Unlike Midas', however, Bottom's fulfillment of desire carries no dangerous consequences—he seems quite content to munch hay and to receive fairyland affection.

As an animated metaphor and as a malapropian character, Bottom represents verbal metamorphosis, the transposition of one word into another. This is part of the power of dramatic art, and imagination is the metamorphic practicer. As the

Ovidian co-star of an Ovidian play-within-a-play following an Ovidian dream experience, Bottom creates his own dramatic tension by attacking his role in accordance with a consistently mimetic theory of theatrical realism.[40] Dream and drama meet but do not mix in Bottom; his imagination is asininely anti-poetic. Shakespeare playfully criticizes Bottom's literalization of art by using his own art to literalize the metaphoric and metamorphic dimensions of his central comic character.

The significance of Bottom *qua* ass to the totality of *A Midsummer Night's Dream*, however, cannot be separated into thematic equivalents or character-delineating functions. Perhaps one must return to the beginning and re-examine Bottom's actual appearance. He is half-man, half-ass, the visual embodiment of Puck's dictum, "what fools these mortals be" (III.ii.115). Accordingly, Bottom serves as a clear comic everyman—a mirror in which the playgoer can see the human condition. As a "licentious ass," he parodies man's half-hidden fascination with the sexual substratum of love. As a "foolish ass," he reflects man's ignorant folly—and its ability to metamorphose into occasional bursts of natural wisdom. As an "admirable ass," he incorporates man's flights into the vatic mysteries of divine revelation and poetic inspiration. Yet his hybrid nature, one radically different from the fluid one exhibited by the other characters in *A Midsummer Night's Dream* who flow from one form or illusion to another, is of signal importance in itself. It suggests the idea of dichotomy per se. In this connection, it symbolizes the primal pattern of the play—the dramatic recreation of the Apollonian-Dionysian dialectic. Theseus' diurnal world represents Apollonian order, whereas Oberon and Puck's nocturnal realm represents Dionysian license.[41] The fact that the ass is sacred to Dionysus and is anathema to Apollo further clarifies Bottom's place in this archetypal scheme.[42] In sum, it was only through the bold and, on the surface, bald-faced use of the ass motif that Shakespeare could economically pack an associational and connotational macrocosm into a humorous microcosm while preserving the structure and the tone of such a comedy as *A Midsummer Night's Dream*.

In the later comedies, Shakespeare discovered other ways in which to present the complex of ideas which the ass motif conveyed in the early 1590s. Chief among these are the emergence of the wise fool, of well-motivated character change, of actualized physical and sexual evil, of a wider range of comic perspective devices, and of the possibility of spiritual transformation. But the early Shakespearean ass, with its ability to contain multitudes without losing its humorous appeal, remains a splendid comic construction.

Notes

1. This is the *OED*'s first listing under "ass" as a term of reproach; the second listing involves "ass" as a vulgarization of the etymologically unrelated word "arse"—a variation of which, as will be shown below, Shakespeare was well aware.

2. According to Martin Spevack's computerized concordance, the word "ass" occurs eighty-eight times in Shakespeare's writings; see *A Complete and Systematic Concordance to the Works of Shakespeare*, IV (Hildesheim: Georg Olms Verlagsbuchhandlung, 1969), p. 357.

3. The information about Plutarch, Tacitus, Tertullian, and Cecilius Felix is found in E. P. Evans, *Animal Symbolism in Ecclesiastical Architecture* (London: 1896; rpt. Detroit: Gale Research, 1969), p. 270.

4. Evans, pp. 267–77. This macaronic liturgy refers to asses as burden-bearers, as chastised sufferers, and as types of Christ; yet one line reads "Asinus egregius." One wonders, in reference to the Shakespearean ass, if Iago recalls this wording when he plans to make Othello "egregiously an ass" (II.i.303). The text cited throughout is *William Shakespeare: The Complete Works*, ed. Alfred Harbage (Baltimore: Penguin, 1975).

5. Geffrey Whitney, *A Choice of Emblemes and Other Devises*, The English Experience, No. 161 (Leyden, 1586; rpt. Amsterdam: Theatrvm Orbis Terrarvm; New York: Da Capo, 1969), p. 8. A modern critic connects this tradition with Apuleius' *The Golden Ass* and notes its conflation with Christ's ass into an image of Christian piety and humility. David Ormerod, "*A Midsummer Night's Dream*: The Monster in the Labyrinth," *Shakespeare Studies*, 11 (1978), 45. See also J. J. M. Tobin, "Apuleius and *Antony and Cleopatra* Once More," *Studia Neophilologica*, 51 (1979), 225–28. For Isis as Diana (and Titania and Bottom as Diana and Actaeon), see Leonard Barkan, "Diana and Actaeon: The Myth as Synthesis," *English Literary Renaissance*, 10 (1980), 317–59. Barkan's study appeared after my article was completed.

6. For instance, Trevisa's translation of Bartholomew's *De proprietatibus rerum* explains that the poor villain, oppressed by the yoke of servitude, can draw consolation from the wretched condition of the ass; it is fair of disposition and shape while it is young, yet becomes "a melancholy beast, that is cold and dry, and therefore kindly, heavy, and slow and unlusty, dull and witless and forgetful. . . ." After being beaten

with staves, the poor animal dies, his body flayed and his carcass left for carrion. This exemplum is cited in Francis Klingender, *Animals in Art and Thought to the End of the Middle Ages*, ed. Evelyn Antal and John Harthan (London: Routledge and Kegan Paul, 1971), pp. 354–58.

7. Publius Ovidius Naso, *Shakespeare's Ovid, Being Arthur Golding's Translation of the Metamorphoses*, ed. W. H. D. Rouse (n.p., 1904; rpt. Carbondale: Southern Illinois Univ. Press, 1961), p. 222. See also Whitney's emblem *Peruersa iudicia*, p. 218 (Fig. 2), which equates Midas' choice with bad judgment in general.

8. Geoffrey Chaucer, *Boece*, in *The Complete Works of Geoffrey Chaucer*, ed. F. N. Robinson (1933; rpt. Boston: Houghton Mifflin, 1957), p. 323. Chaucer explained his conception of the proverb's significance when he used it in *Troilus and Criseyde* (quoted from Robinson edition). Pandarus asks Troilus:

"What! slombrest ow as in a litargie?

Or artow lik an asse to the harpe,

That hereth sown whan men the strynges plye,

But in his mynde of that no melodie

May sinken hym to gladen, for that he

So dul ys of his bestialite?"

(I.730–35)

9. Chaucer, *Boece*, p. 363.
10. Whitney, p. 82.
11. Ormerod, p. 46, reports that Ripa explained: "La testa dell Asino mostra la medesima l'ignoranza"; similarly, he cites Valeriano's gloss (p. 52, note 28): "ces bons gens de prestres par la test d'Ane mise sur un tronc de corps humain, signifioyent l'homme ignorant ... l'Asne est l'hieroglyphique d'ignorance."
12. This tradition evidently dates to antiquity; there exists a terra cotta figure of a Roman mime wearing a close-fitting eared hood. Robert Hillis Goldsmith, *Wise Fools in Shakespeare* (Liverpool: Liverpool Univ. Press, 1958), p. 2.
13. Desiderius Erasmus, *The Praise of Folie*, trans. Sir Thomas Chaloner, ed. Clarence H. Miller, Early English Text Society Publications, Orig. Ser., No. 257 (London: Oxford Univ. Press, 1965), p. 10. The two subsequent references to this work will appear in the text.
14. Sebastian Brant, *The Ship of Fools*, trans. Alexander Barclay (Edinburgh, 1874; rpt. New York: AMS, 1966), I, 181, 156–57, 248.
15. See E. A. M. Colman, *The Dramatic Use of Bawdy in Shakespeare* (London: Longman, 1974), pp. 41, 217; Eric Partridge, *Shakespeare's Bawdy* (New York: Dutton, 1955), pp. 67, 200. The simple pun occurs in *King Lear* (I.iv. 152–54), where "ass/arse" is paired with the concept of fool. A similar constellation occurs in act I, scene i of *Cymbeline*. Note the pictorial emphasis upon the ass's posteriors in Figure 5.
16. Beryl Rowland, *Animals with Human Faces: A Guide to Animal Symbolism* (Knoxville: Univ. of Tennessee Press, 1973), p. 21. Also, note the position of the woman's head in relation to the ass's rump in Figure 4.
17. See Ezekiel xxiii.19; for the ass as an Egyptian, Greek, and Hindu symbol of lust, see Rowland, pp. 23–24.

18. William Adlington, trans., *The Golden Ass*, by Apuleius, ed. S. Gaselee (1915; rpt. Cambridge, Mass.: Harvard Univ. Press, 1947), p. xvi.

19. T. W. Baldwin (*On the Compositional Genetics of The Comedy of Errors* [Urbana: Univ. of Illinois Press, 1965], pp. 166–67) also notes the biblical wording of this passage and connects it with homiletic literature concerning the state of matrimony. In addition, see Richard Henze, "*The Comedy of Errors*: A Freely Binding Chain," *Shakespeare Quarterly*, 22 (1971), 37.

20. The physical abuse stems in part from Plautus. The *Menaechmi* presents episodes in which the actors are beaten like beasts; the *Amphitruo* brims with thrashings, kicks, and blows. The only actual use of the word "ass," however, occurs in the fourth act of the *Menaechmi* as the furious Citizen Menechmus calls the parasite an "Asse." Here the word merely signifies an ignorant fool. See Geoffrey Bullough, ed., *Narrative and Dramatic Sources of Shakespeare*, I (London: Routledge and Kegan Paul, 1957), 12–39, 40–49. Perhaps as he was working with classical sources Shakespeare recalled the title of another Plautine play, *Asinaria*, which is concerned with the ridicule of a foolish master by an outrageous slave. A more likely inspiration for the equation of servants with asses is Lyly's *Mother Bombie*, in which the impudent servant Dromio is called an ass by his master and by his fellow slaves. See John Lyly, *Mother Bombie*, in *The Complete Writings of John Lyly*, ed. R. Warwick Bond, III (1902; rpt. Oxford: Clarendon, 1967), 173, 185.

21. It seems that Shakespeare changed the *Menaechmi*'s Epidamnum to Ephesus in order to allude to the supernatural aura that pervaded the city in acts xix. See Baldwin, pp. 51, 65–66; Harold Brooks, "Theme and Structure in *The Comedy of Errors*," in *Early Shakespeare*, ed. J. R. Brown and B. Harris (London: Edward Arnold, 1961); rpt. in *Shakespeare, The Comedies: A Collection of Critical Essays*, ed. Kenneth Muir (Englewood Cliffs, N.J.: Prentice-Hall, 1965), p. 20. Furthermore, the change points to the passage in Ephesians which describes the duty one owes to proper societal relationships between master and servant, husband and wife. Bullough, p. 9.

22. The editor of the New Arden edition of the play also distinguishes the metamorphic theme and sees it operating as an indicator of psychological disturbance: "Each Dromio applies the term 'ass' to the beatings he is made to suffer, and to the way he is made to seem a fool; but the idea of being made a beast operates more generally in the play, reflecting the process of passion overcoming reason, as an animal rage, fear, or spite seizes on each of the main characters." R. A. Foakes, ed., *The Comedy of Errors*. The Arden Shakespeare (London: Methuen, 1962), p. xiv. Northrop Frye (*A Natural Perspective: The Development of Shakespearean Comedy and Romance* [New York: Columbia Univ. Press, 1965], pp. 106–7) believes that "[t]he structure of *The Comedy of Errors* is a metamorphic structure, a descent into illusion and an emergence into recognition."

23. Frye, p. 106, calls the speech a view of "what the human world would look like to a conscious ass: an inferno of malignant and purposeless beating." Ralph Berry (*Shakespeare's Comedies: Explorations in Form* [Princeton: Princeton Univ. Press, 1972], p. 34) agrees; he writes that this existential *cri de coeur* "is the sharply caught apprehension of what it must be like to be a servant in a world of mad masters, to be sane and yet in an impotent minority."

24. Ifor Evans (*The Language of Shakespeare's Plays* [London: Methuen, 1966], p. 10), calling metaphor "the applied metaphysic of poetry," states that its magnetic action "asserts the unity of human life." Correspondingly, Bottom, a metaphoric character *par excellence*, is the focus of the unity of the play. Similarly, David

Young (*Something of Great Constancy: The Art of A Midsummer Night's Dream* [New Haven: Yale Univ. Press, 1966], p. 92) finds Bottom at the center of the play's concentric circles of action. Bottom may even be a visual pun, if Partridge, p. 78, is correct in thinking that "bottom" could signify the human posteriors to an Elizabethan audience. Colman, p. 28, disagrees, however, and the *OED* gives 1794 as the date of its first example of this particular usage.

25. Sister M. Generosa, "Apuleius and *A Midsummer Night's Dream*: Analogue or Source, Which?" *Studies in Philology*, 42 (1945), 200.

26. See John A. Allen, "Bottom and Titania," *Shakespeare Quarterly*, 18 (1967), 107.

27. Melvin Goldstein, "Identity Crisis in A Midsummer Nightmare: Comedy as Terror in Disguise," *The Psychoanalytic Review*, 60 (1973), 175; Jan Kott, *Shakespeare Our Contemporary*, trans. Boleslaw Taborski (Garden City, N.Y.: Doubleday, 1964), p. 218.

28. Bruno Bettelheim (*The Uses of Enchantment: The Meaning and Importance of Fairy Tales* [New York: Knopf, 1976], pp. 306–9), stresses the positive aspects of the archetype. In contrast, C. L. Barber (*Shakespeare's Festive Comedy: A Study of Dramatic Form and its Relation to Social Custom* [Princeton: Princeton Univ. Press, 1959], p. 155) states that Bottom and Titania portray "fancy against fact, not beauty and the beast."

29. See Willard Farnham, *The Shakespearean Grotesque: Its Genesis and Transformation* (Oxford: Clarendon, 1971), pp. 12, 32, for a discussion of the comedy of the grotesque; Farnham does not analyze Bottom in these terms.

30. Ormerod, p. 40, presents the idea that Shakespeare deliberately transformed the Theseus and the Minotaur myth, substituting a symbol of funny foolishness for one of bestial passion and a maze-like woods for the Cretan Labyrinth.

31. Thelma N. Greenfield, "*A Midsummer Night's Dream* and *The Praise of Folly*" *Comparative Literature*, 20 (1968), 239.

32. Lyly, *Midas* (IV.i), in *The Complete Works of John Lyly*, p. 144.

33. Many critics have made this point. See Barber, p. 148; Young, p. 103. Also applicable is Reginald Scot's marginal note to his account in *The Discoverie of Witchcraft* of the young man changed into an ass by a witch (quoted in Bullough, pp. 401–3): "A strange metamorphosis of body, but not of mind."

34. Greenfield, p. 240, states rather broadly that men feel a sympathetic camaraderie with asses and, therefore, with Bottom.

35. James L. Calderwood, *Shakespearean Metadrama* (Minneapolis: Univ. of Minnesota Press, 1971), p. 56.

36. Ronald F. Miller ("*A Midsummer Night's Dream*: The Fairies, Bottom, and the Mystery of Things," *Shakespeare Quarterly*, 26 [1975], 265–66) draws this parallel between the name and function of the weaver and the Tyndale translation of I Cor. ii.6–10. See also Andrew D. Weiner ("'Multiformitie Uniforme': *A Midsummer Night's Dream*," *ELH*, 38 [1971], 347), and J. Dennis Huston ("Bottom Waking: Shakespeare's 'Most Rare Vision,'" *Studies in English Literature*, 13 [1973], 212–14). Thomas B. Stroup ("Bottom's Name and His Epiphany," *Shakespeare Quarterly*, 29 [1978], 79–82) agrees that this speech is a short but profound epiphany experienced by a wise fool; however, Robert F. Willson, Jr. ("God's Secrets and Bottom's Name: A Reply," *Shakespeare Quarterly*, 30 [1979], 407–8) warns against transforming Bottom's vision into a morality play.

37. John Russell Brown, *Shakespeare and his Comedies* (London: Methuen, 1957), p. 84.

38. See Barber, p. 133; Walter F. Staton, Jr. ("Ovidian Elements in *A Midsummer Night's Dream*," *Huntington Library Quarterly*, 26 [1962–63], 166–68); and Madeleine Doran (*Endeavors of Art: A Study of Form in Elizabethan Drama* [Madison: Univ. of Wisconsin Press, 1954], p. 293).
39. See Young, p. 157.
40. Jackson I. Cope, *The Theater and the Dream* (Baltimore: Johns Hopkins Univ. Press, 1973), p. 222. Cope explores dream, imagination, and theatre in *A Midsummer Night's Dream*, as does James L. Calderwood "*A Midsummer Night's Dream*: The Illusion of Drama," *Modern Language Quarterly*, 26 [1965], 507), who writes that the play is "part of Shakespeare's continuing exploration of the nature, function, and value of art."
41. See Neil D. Isaacs and Jack E. Reese, "Dithyramb and Paean in *A Midsummer Night's Dream*," *English Studies*, 55 (1974), 351–57. The authors' thesis seems to be based largely on Barber.
42. Helen Adolf ("The Ass and the Harp," *Speculum*, 25 [1950], 50–54) gives the classical ass analogues and briefly places Bottom in the tradition, but stresses that he becomes part of a vast "naturally cosmic" order as well.

A Midsummer Night's Dream Exposes Taboo Sexuality

Bruce Boehrer

Bruce Boehrer is a professor of English at Florida State University. He is also the author of several books, including Animal Characters: Nonhuman Beings in Early Modern Literature; Parrot Culture: Our 2500-Year-Long Fascination with the World's Most Talkative Bird; *and* Shakespeare Among the Animals: Nature and Society in the Drama of Early Modern England.

Bruce Boehrer cites textual evidence for allusions to homosociality and bestiality that appear throughout Shakespeare's A Midsummer Night's Dream. *Boehrer points to the formation of same-sex relationships that are formed between Hermia and Helena. Both homosexuality and bestiality are alluded to in the story of Nick Bottom and his fellow mechanicals. In this all-male theatrical society, Bottom enthusiastically asks to play the lion's part where he tests the limits both of species and of gender. By exposing taboo sexuality, Shakespeare problematizes the idea of traditional marriage.*

Over the past two decades, scholars have grown increasingly interested in two seemingly unrelated patterns of reference in Shakespeare's *A Midsummer Night's Dream* (ca. 1596). On one hand, they have encountered a string of allusions to cross-species eroticism that, when taken collectively, may be read as a correlative to the play's language of patriarchal hegemony. On the other hand, they have discerned an undercurrent of sexual reference in the play that foregrounds various sorts of same-sex attachment. . . .

Bruce Boehrer, "Economies of Desire in *A Midsummer Night's Dream*," *Shakespeare Studies*, vol. 32, 2004, pp. 99–117. Copyright © 2004 by Associated University Presses. All rights reserved. Reproduced by permission.

Same-Sex Relationships

A parallel same-sex formulation, occurring within moments of Hippolyta's first appearance onstage, supplies the structural discriminations within which Hermia's, Helena's, Lysander's, and Demetrius's sexual choices take on meaning; subject to her father Egeus's will and to the law of Athens, Hermia must either wed Demetrius or, alternatively, "endure the livery of a nun, / For aye to be in shady cloister mewed, / To live a barren sister all [her] life, / Chanting faint hymns to the cold fruitless moon" (I.i.70–73). The choice here—reconfiguring Egeus's original ultimatum of marriage or death (I.i.41–45)—takes shape primarily as a contrast between cross-gendered fecundity and homosocial childlessness, which serves as the genealogical and sexual equivalent of execution. This, again, is generally how the opposition reappears in act 3, scene 2, as Helena distinguishes between her long-standing friendship with Hermia and the latter's apparently heartless decision to betray that friendship by joining Lysander and Demetrius in their mockery of her friend's loveless solitude:

Injurious Hermia, most ungrateful maid,

Have you conspired, have you with these contrived,

To bate me with this foul derision?

Is all the counsel that we two have shared—

The sisters' vows, the hours that we have spent

When we have chid the hasty-footed time

For parting us—O, is all quite forgot?

All school-days' friendship, childhood innocence?

We, Hermia, like two artificial gods

> Have with our needles created both one flower,
>
> Both on one sampler, sitting on one cushion,
>
> Both warbling of one song, both in one key,
>
> As if our hands, our sides, voices, and minds,
>
> Had been incorporate.
>
> (III.ii.196–209)

Here, once more, heterosexual and homosocial unions acquire the character of a categorical opposition, with Hermia's apparent perfidy defined precisely by her investment in the former and her concomitant repudiation of the latter. It is a move from one sort of "incorporation"—the idyllic union about which Helena reminisces bitterly—to another: the union of husband and wife as one flesh that Helena believes to be prefigured in Hermia's emotional estrangement and antagonistic mockery. Likewise, it is a move from one sort of reproduction to another—from the "artificial" creativity of Helena and Hermia's sampler, with its likeness of the living world, to the organic creativity of parenthood, which has earlier been given a peculiarly artificial figuration in Theseus's advice to Hermia:

> To you your father should be as a god,
>
> One that composed your beauties, yea, and one
>
> To whom you are but as a form in wax
>
> By him imprinted, and within his power
>
> To leave the figure, or disfigure it.
>
> (I.i.47–51)

Sexuality in *A Midsummer Night's Dream*

The opposition of parenthood to artifice, and of heteroerotic to homosocial union, thus takes form both through mutual exclusion and through mutual imitation, as a progression of artificial gods that calls notice, inevitably, to the artificiality of the gestures whereby they counter and yet mimic one another.

This specular opposition receives its most obvious embodiment, in turn, in the most obvious of Shakespeare's plots: the story of [Nick] Bottom and his fellow mechanicals. Here, within a guild society that famously reproduces the all-male context of Shakespearean theatrical production, Bottom distinguishes himself from his comrades by a histrionic zeal that exceeds the limits both of species and of gender: "An I may hide my face, let me play Thisbe. . . . Let me play the lion too. I will roar that I will do any man's heart good to hear me" [I.ii.43, 58–59]. The range of his theatrical aspirations may mark Bottom as a figure of greater than ordinary imaginative gifts, but this distinction, in turn, need not be regarded as a self-evidently good thing. By contrast, Flute and Snug—the designated Thisbe and Lion of Bottom's company—display no such enthusiasm for their roles, and understandably not, given the threat such roles represent to the principle of masculine, and human, identity upon which their guild community is centered. Where Snug, being by his own admission "slow of study," worries about his capacity to learn the lion's lines (I.ii.55–56), Flute seeks unsuccessfully to avoid being cast as Thisbe by protesting that he has "a beard coming" (I.ii.39–40). And rightly so, given the upshot: as Thisbe and Pyramus lie dead in the fifth act of Shakespeare's comedy, thereby becoming the play's only staged casualties, one is confronted with a particularly graphic instance of the pervasive incompatibility *A Midsummer Night's Dream* posits between its same-gender and cross-gender communities. If, for Theseus, life in a nunnery figures as the functional equivalent of death, so, for the mechanicals, does wedlock. . . .

Cross-Species Encounters

Moments of homosociality and bestiality recur throughout *A Midsummer Night's Dream* in something like a calculated pattern of balance and antithesis. Hippolyta's former status as Queen of the Amazons plays against her current status as war prize and her etymological affiliation with horses. Helena and Hermia's inveterate friendship plays against Helena's self-denigration as Demetrius's "spaniel," and also against Puck's blanket assurance to the young lovers that "The man shall have his mare again"—which declaration speaks in turn to the play's earlier threat of cloistered celibacy for Hermia. As for Bottom's curious dismay over the defloration of his dear (a dismay expressed, one might also note, as he holds aloft her bloodied mantle [V.i.271–72]), it contrasts with the same-sex exclusivity of the artisanal community that produces it. Taking a cue from Lysander's words to Demetrius at I.i.93–94, we might observe that oppositions of this sort recur around the central subject of wedlock, and we might conjecture that such recurrence comprises one of the play's symbolic resources for accommodating the anxieties its subject matter elicits, both for its characters and for its audiences. Certainly, according to Lysander's formulation of things, the principle of masculine homosocial authority comprises a threat to any notion of wedlock grounded in cross-gender attraction and mutual acceptance, and the various women's communities evoked by the play (Hippolyta's Amazon sisterhood, Hermia's nunnery, and the girlhood friendship of Helena and Hermia, for example) seem equally uncongenial to heteronormative marital behavior. Where these social configurations agree in their general commitment to the erasure of gender difference, Shakespeare's discourse of bestiality, on the other hand, confronts alterity head-on by translating it from gender to species. The result is a series of formulations that complement the residual absolutism of patriarchal marriage in *A Midsummer Night's Dream*: moments when the traditional division between humankind and brute nature is conscripted into the discourse of masculine hegemony by depicting Helena as spaniel, for instance, or by suggesting that wife is to husband as mare is to man. But likewise, these moments recall the unease Shakespeare's comedy displays toward the potential extremes of patriarchal absolutism represented by Egeus's treatment of his daughter, for the bestiality motif in *A Midsummer Night's Dream* serves as a graphic reminder that difference cannot be fantasized out of the heteronormative marital bond. To this extent, the hybrid coupling of human being and beast figures the return of the patriarchal repressed.

If, then, the bestiality motif in *A Midsummer Night's Dream* operates as a structural and phantasmatic counterpart to the play's preoccupation with same-sex relationships, its function as such centers upon Titania's infatuation with Bottom. And Bottom's asinine character seems ideally devised to foreground issues of alterity and hybridity. For not only does the ass figure in the bestiary tradition as a vehicle for various sorts of hermeneutic *coincidentiae oppositorum*, but it famously performs the same function in the flesh as well. Early natural historians dwell at length on the process of breeding mules by mating asses to mares, and they describe this procedure in ways that bear on both the structural and social dimensions of Titania's encounter with Bottom. Thus Aelian observes that

> The Horse is generally speaking a proud creature, ... [b]ut it is chiefly a Mare with a long mane that is so full of airs and graces. For instance, she scorns to be covered by an ass, but is glad to mate with a horse, regarding herself as only fit for the greatest of her kind. Accordingly, those who wish to have mules born, knowing this characteristic, clip the Mare's mane in a haphazard fashion anyhow, and then put asses to her. Though ashamed at first, she admits her present ignoble mate. Sophocles also appears to mention this humiliation.

More than merely a practical act of animal husbandry, the process of cross-mating emerges from this description as something like an exercise in attitude adjustment: a calculated "humiliation" that corrects the mare's prideful contempt for otherness. Given the equine metaphors that occasionally apply to Shakespeare's feminine characters in *A Midsummer Night's Dream*, the correspondence between this act of corrective humiliation and the embarrassment of Titania's infatuation with Bottom may almost seem deliberate (although, of course, the present analysis relies on no such assumption). In any case, the passionate conjunction of woman and ass draws attention, through the latter's common association with cross-species mating, to the broad structural significance of the bestiality motif it embodies. . . .

Patriarchal Society and Marriage

Hence the core of my argument in this [viewpoint]: the theme of bestiality in *A Midsummer Night's Dream*, most graphically represented by Titania's interlude with the asinine Bottom, lends overt expression to the play's uneasiness with gender difference and its inevitable role in the development of reproductive marital sexuality. However, the play's concurrent emphasis upon same-sex union, which even extends to the fantasy of a patriarchal authoritarian marriage committed at least to the symbolic (if not actually the physical) erasure of the feminine, emerges as equally unsatisfactory and equally anxiety provoking. Caught as she is between her changeling page and her assified lover, Titania enacts an uneasy transition from the latter state to the former. In the process, she illustrates the discomforts associated respectively with these competing states of homocentric and heterocentric affection, and she reveals the interconnection between these discomforts and the paired themes of same-sex union and of bestiality that lend them expression in her play.

To this extent, Titania's choice between Bottom and the Indian page exemplifies the economies of desire that structure *A Midsummer Night's Dream* as a whole. Most broadly, these may be characterized as the competing impulses to embrace and to repudiate alterity. On the practical level, these impulses achieve their most obvious accommodation—and ironically, come into most direct conflict—relative to the play's various depictions of patriarchal wedlock. As for the accommodation, it is obvious enough: Theseus may have subdued Hippolyta, but she scarcely seems displeased about the arrangement; Titania freely yields up her page to Oberon and returns contentedly to his bed; the young lovers marry according to their affections, in a configuration sanctioned by ducal authority; Bottom and his comrades get to perform—and are rewarded for performing—an interlude to celebrate the weddings of their betters. In each of these cases, alterity seems to be happily encompassed within conventions of courtly and familial behavior that privilege the masculine homosocial over the heteroerotic.

But the play's conflicts still persist; despite these final felicities, *A Midsummer Night's Dream* "seems rather to *problematize* than to celebrate marriage." Theseus authorizes the wedding of Lysander and Hermia only by exceeding what he himself has identified as the limits of his legal writ as duke, overruling the will of an outraged father who insists upon the ancient patriarchal privileges of Athens. For their part, the quarto texts of *A Midsummer Night's Dream* conspicuously exclude this father from the nuptials with which the play ends, and which mark the triumph of his daughter's will over his own. But perhaps most importantly, the play's various accommodations between its competing principles of homophilia and heterophilia are consistently managed in defiance of, rather than in obedience to, the spirit of probability. If Hippolyta is reconciled to Theseus, one feels that it can only be by the same mechanism that reconciles Titania to Oberon and Demetrius to Helena: the gratuitous and superrational intervention of magic. In this sense, one could say that *A Midsummer Night's Dream* ultimately lacks faith in its own festive conclusion, suggesting, thus, the darker tone of Shakespearean comedies to come.

This point, finally, may recall the waggish truism that Shakespearean comedy ends in marriage because that is where Shakespearean tragedy begins. As Ruth Nevo has observed, "marriage partners must maintain their distinctive personalities, recognize each other's and enter into a new corporate personality, or transaction of personalities." Yet, as Nevo has argued, the erotic unions of *A Midsummer Night's Dream* are in constant peril of devolving from this ideal state of cooperation into a concomitant state of rivalry. One function of the play's juxtaposed patterns of bestiality and homosociality is arguably to embody the anxieties—of encounter with the other, of confinement to the self—from which such rivalry can arise. And indeed, one may wonder just how thoroughly Nevo's ideal of marital cooperation applies to an historical context so committed to patriarchal authority and domestic hierarchy as was Shakespeare's. In the end, *A Midsummer Night's Dream* seems more nervous than reassuring, less convinced of its own happy fantasies than aware of their evanescence. As delightful as it may be, the play's escapism is a little too self-conscious, and its alternatives a little too dark, for comfort. If, as the wag says, Shakespearean marriage is a prelude to tragedy, *A Midsummer Night's Dream* is a prelude to the darker Shakespearean plays that follow.

Shakespeare's Defiant Daughters Affirm a New Morality

Diane Elizabeth Dreher

Diane Elizabeth Dreher is a professor of English at Santa Clara University. Among her books are The Fourfold Pilgrimage: The Estates of Innocence, Misery, Grace, and Glory in Seventeenth-Century Literature *and* The Tao of Inner Peace.

Dreher places Hermia from A Midsummer Night's Dream *in the Shakespearean galaxy of daughters who defy their fathers' wishes, and, in a "crisis of intimacy," choose to create their own identity rather than be defined by others. Hermia refuses to marry her father's chosen suitor, and in doing so moves from a static character to a dynamic one who actively searches for her own adult commitment. Dreher writes that in rejecting the arranged union with Demetrius, Hermia rejects the woman's traditional role as the husband's sexual slave. Through her ordeal, and those of Shakespearean daughters like her, she casts off the old social order and creates a new, more personal morality of her own. Though Hermia does not have her father's blessing, Dreher suggests, she certainly has Shakespeare's.*

Seventeen of Shakespeare's plays address the crisis of intimacy, when daughters leave their fathers for the commitment of marriage. This creates identity crises for them as well as for their parents. In what [psychologist Erik] Erikson has seen as "the stage of life crucial for the emergence of an integrated female identity," young women leave behind the secure bonds of childhood and go forth into the unknown, risking

---

Diane Elizabeth Dreher, *Domination and Defiance: Fathers and Daughters in Shakespeare*, 1986, pp. 96–101. Copyright © 1986 by University Press of Kentucky. All rights reserved. Reproduced by permission.

lifelong commitment to a stranger in the adventure of awakening love. Most of Shakespeare's daughters defy their fathers to make this commitment, actively affirming new values and priorities. With the sole exception of Ophelia [a character in Shakespeare's *Hamlet*], once their hearts are touched by romantic love, these young women embrace it as their destiny, rejecting patriarchal bonds and childhood commitments. In this [viewpoint] I shall examine the defiance of [*A Midsummer Night's Dream's*] Hermia, [*Two Gentlemen of Verona's*] Silvia, . . . [Othello's] Desdemona, [*Cymbeline's*] Imogen, [and] *The Merry Wives of Windsor's* Anne Page. . . . All leave behind traditional filial obedience, affirming something new in its place. Some move from what [American professor Carol] Gilligan called "a focus on goodness . . . to a reflective understanding of care as the most adequate guide to resolution of conflicts in human relationships." Unlike [*Much Ado About Nothing's*] Hero and Desdemona, these young women are able to care for themselves as well as others, moving from the dependence of childhood to interdependence and an affirmation of human community. Their defiance constitutes part of a comic pattern of thesis, antithesis, synthesis, which leads to new social harmony. . . .

Romantic love takes young women from childhood to adulthood. It is [according to Erikson] "a crucial moment, when development must move one way or another, marshalling resources of growth, recovery, and further differentiation." This developmental crisis and its effects—the daughter's revolt, the father's reaction, and the values affirmed—form the structural core of at least nine tragedies and comedies. Daughters in these plays choose love over paternal obedience, affirming personal choice over enforced duty. Yet while Shakespeare dramatized the limits of traditional order, he recognized the need for other bonds to prevent its opposite, rampant greed and social chaos. In his plays he consistently condemns both slavish obedience and unbridled appetite, upholding a personal bond of love and trust as the only moral basis for enduring human commitment.

Trial by Ordeal

In Shakespeare's romantic comedies, the daughters' defiance leads to personal and social renewal.... In the archetypal conflict that develops youthful dreams into adult commitments, parents must play the rigid role of authority, upholding an order against which young people can exercise their emerging sense of self. Paternal authority provides the initial thesis in this developmental dialectic of personal growth and social renewal.

Like [English poet] John Milton a few decades later, Shakespeare recognized that human development arises through conflict, that in challenge we strengthen and define ourselves: "That which purifies us is trial, and trial is by what is contrary." Shakespeare's concern is developmental, his concept of adulthood surprisingly modern. His daughters are not static ideals but dynamic characters who actively search for adult commitment. Love for them is a process of growth in which they discover a new sense of self and affirm a value system based on mutual respect and trust.

Hermia's Defiance

Shakespeare dramatized this clash of traditional and progressive perspectives in I.i of *A Midsummer Night's Dream*. In answer to her father's insistence that she marry Demetrius, Hermia declares, "I would my father look'd but with my eyes." Literally, she argues for her point of view; the man she loves is Lysander. Figuratively, she stands for the progressive view of marriage: not a dispassionate family arrangement, but a personal commitment between two individuals. Speaking for traditional authority, Theseus counsels, "Rather your eyes must with his judgement look" (I.i.56–57). In keeping with the fifth commandment, a daughter was to let her father's judgment determine her actions. Traditionalists prized obedience over reason and initiative, while humanists and Puritans defined virtue more actively. Empowered by her love, Hermia speaks to the duke as Desdemona does in *Othello*. Rejecting the silent passive model of female virtue, she dares to make her own decisions. Like Renaissance scientists, she refuses to accept established authority, considering all available data before reaching her own conclusion. Hermia realizes that her behavior is unconventional. She apologizes for her seeming breach of modesty while inquiring about the penalty for disobedience:

> I do entreat your grace to pardon me.
>
> I know not by what power I am made bold,
>
> Nor how it may concern my modesty,
>
> In such a presence here to plead my thoughts;
>
> But I beseech your grace that I may know
>
> The worst that may befall me in this case,
>
> If I refuse to wed Demetrius. [I.i.58–64]

Learning that her alternatives are death and perpetual celibacy, she affirms her integrity, refusing to be a mere property passed from father to husband. She will not let an unloved man possess her body:

> So will I grow, so live, so die, my lord,
>
> Ere I will yield my virgin patent up
>
> Unto his lordship, whose unwished yoke
>
> My soul consents not to give sovereignty.
>
> [I.i.79–82]

Hermia rejects forced marriage to "his lordship," the "unwished yoke" and "sovereignty" of traditional arranged marriage in which women too often became their husbands' sexual slaves. She affirms her right to consent, echoing Renaissance Puritans, who enabled young women to veto their father's choice, choosing to obey God over their fathers. As Gilligan explained, "the concept of rights changes a woman's conceptions of self, allowing them to see themselves as stronger and to consider directly their own needs," changing personal relationships "from a bond of continuing dependence to a dynamic of interdependence."

Hermia later escapes with Lysander from the tyranny of Athenian law. Their elopement leads them, along with Helena and Demetrius, through a surrealistic ordeal in the woods, which teaches them that love can be threatened, not only externally but internally. They must temper their passions and overcome adolescent egotism to make an adult commitment. In IV.i they awaken to a new vision. Hermia sees "with parted eye, / When every thing seems double" (IV.i.193–94). Through their ordeal they overcome the egocentric illusions of adolescence, the young men's need to prove themselves in competition for the most desirable young woman, and the young women's insecurities about their attractiveness. Seeing beyond tradition, illusion, and appearance, they develop their faith in a love they cannot rationally explain.

Silvia and Desdemona

Silvia in the early *Two Gentlemen of Verona* is another progressive young woman. Like Desdemona, she initiates the courtship, asking Valentine to write a love letter to an unnamed friend, then presenting it to Valentine himself. Although her jealous father locks her up in a tower at night, she plans to elope with Valentine, using a rope ladder. After Proteus reveals their plan, Silvia remains loyal, rejecting the advances of her father's wealthy favorite and the inconstant Proteus, whom she lectures on his infidelity to Julia. She then runs away to join Valentine in Mantua, demonstrating courage and commitment. In some rather unbelievable turns of plot,

In many of Shakespeare's plays, the theme of daughters defying their parents for love can be seen. In Romeo and Juliet, *both teens defy their parents to be together, though their defiance ends in tragedy with both of their deaths.* © Bettmann/Corbis.

this comedy concludes with affirmations of friendship and forgiveness, matching each young man with his original lady and obtaining the blessing of Silvia's father.

In what resembles a comic plot, Desdemona defies her father to affirm her love for Othello. Her elopement trumpets to the world the depth of her love, demonstrating individual choice, courage, and commitment. But in this tragic world there is no father's blessing to bring the lovers back into society. There is only Brabantio's warning, a bitter parody. In marrying Othello, Desdemona has divorced her family and country. Her father disowns her and dies in despair, as she goes with Othello to an alien land. In her new role as wife, she clings to the ideal of traditional womanhood, pathetically accepting Othello's verbal and physical abuse with sweetness, patience, and passivity. Her attempts at wifely obedience and feminine perfection ironically ally with Iago's efforts to undermine the trust essential for intimacy. A victim of cross purposes and impossible ideals, Desdemona is caught squarely in the transition between traditional and progressive concepts of marriage and womanhood.

Juliet

Juliet is another tragic heroine whose love begins with the familiar pattern of comic defiance. The young lovers are at odds with their elders, who function as *alazons* [imposters], their feud creating impediments to young love. Critics emphasize the fact that love matures Juliet, turning her almost overnight from a child to a woman. For [critic] Irene Dash, Juliet's youth gives her additional independence, for she has not yet accepted the docile, subordinate role of the traditional woman that girls accept when they grow older. I would not attribute Juliet's independence to her youth, however.... Women were indoctrinated from childhood with submission and obedience. Children, male and female, were considered their parents' property. The only difference was that one day boys grew up, while girls remained docile and obedient children, the virtues of the good child and the good woman being almost synonymous.

Juliet develops from her first appearance in I.iii, when we see her as a child who comes at her mother's command and considers marriage "an honour that I dream not of" (65). What develops her independence and maturity is her love for Romeo. She is willing to listen to Paris's offer, but once she exchanges her true love's vows with Romeo, she is committed irrevocably to the love that rules her life. No longer a child, she accepts the world of adult commitment and sexuality, taking the initiative and proposing to Romeo in II.ii. Once married, she anticipates her love's consummation in III.ii, her young blood stirring in a manner that would distress other less sanguine maidens. Like Hermia, she reserves the right to commit herself and her body to the man of her choice. She later affirms her love beyond any ties of family loyalty or childhood security. With a burst of indignation, she rejects her nurse's offer of bigamy and maintains her fidelity to Romeo. At fourteen, abandoned by all she has ever known, this is courage indeed. Ultimately, she chooses union with Romeo in death over the friar's offer of life in a convent. Rejecting all compromise, she upholds love as the basis of her existence. In her courageous defiance of convention for love, Juliet resembles the young women of romantic comedy, but her love blossoms in a tragic universe, a world poisoned by hate, in which there can be no redemption, only *anagnorisis* [a moment of discovery] and remorse.

Imogen and Anne Page

Imogen in *Cymbeline* is another defiant daughter who chooses love over filial obedience. As the play opens, she has incurred her father's displeasure but has won the admiration of the court by rejecting the foolish Cloten for the more worthy Posthumus. Cymbeline banishes Posthumus and imprisons Imogen, calling her a "disloyal thing" (I.i.131) and encouraging Cloten to court her. Throughout these indignities and the greater trials that follow, Imogen affirms her love. She tells her father, "I am senseless of your wrath; a touch more rare / Subdues all pangs, all fears" (I.i.135–36). Like the other young women discussed in this section, she regards marriage not as an arrangement to please her father, but as a personal commitment. She claims Posthumus as her soul mate, in the progressive spirit advocated by Puritans, explaining to Cymbeline, "You bred him as my playfellow, and he is / A man worth any woman" (I.i.145–46). She repels the advances of Cloten and the temptations of Iachimo, running off to meet Posthumus in Milford Haven, where even the plot against her life cannot quench her love. Donning a page's garments, she follows her heart through fantastic adventures in the forest and finally returns to claim her husband and receive her father's blessing. Faithful in love despite the thousand shocks she encounters, Imogen merits the name of her alter ego: Fidele.

Romantic love in the comedies is an irresistible force, inexplicable as grace itself, which draws young people into marriage, providing them with a partner for life. These plays reflect the Puritan definition of love as a gift of God, a force of inspiration and renewal. In *The Merry Wives of Windsor*, Anne Page elopes with [the young gentlemen] Fenton, rejecting the suitors her parents have chosen. Fenton's speech in V.v articulates the progressive view of marriage:

> You would have married her most shamefully,
>
> Where there was no proportion held in love.
>
> The truth is, she and I, long since contracted,
>
> Are now so sure that nothing can dissolve us.
>
> Th'offence is holy that she hath committed;
>
> And this deceit loses the name of craft,
>
> Of disobedience, or unduteous title,

> Since therein she doth evitate and shun
>
> A thousand irreligious cursed hours,
>
> Which forced marriage would have brought upon her.
>
> [Vv. 235–43]

"Th'offence is holy that she hath committed"—consistently Shakespeare moves beyond the plot machinations of new comedy and portrays romantic love as a matter of conscience over parental obedience. As [English theologians] William Gouge ... and Thomas Gataker had argued, children were not to obey their parents in anything contrary to true religion. In choosing to follow her heart, Anne Page "shun[ned] / A thousand irreligious cursed hours" in the hell of a forced marriage. Repeatedly, Shakespeare's daughters reject the old order and affirm a new, more personal morality.

A Midsummer Night's Dream: "Jack shall have Jill; / Nought shall go ill"

Shirley Nelson Garner

Shirley Nelson Garner is a professor at the University of Minnesota where she specializes in Renaissance literature, feminist studies, and Shakespeare. Her books include Antifeminism in the Academy *and* Shakespearean Tragedy and Gender.

Garner finds A Midsummer Night's Dream *to be a sexist play, where male fulfillment depends on the submission of the main female characters. Furthermore, beneath the obvious romantic relationships in the play, patriarchs such as Oberon, Theseus, and Egeus pursue homoerotic attachments with, respectively, the Indian boy, the Amazonian—and masculine—Hippolyta, and Demetrius. The males' happiness is posited on dividing the women in the play and bonding with the other males. Thus erstwhile friends Hermia and Helena quarrel and break apart during their night in the forest. Garner argues that the happy resolution comes at the expense of women, who are largely silent and subdued at the play's end.*

Jack shall have Jill;

Nought shall go ill;

The man shall have his mare again,

and all shall be well.[1]

More than any of Shakespeare's comedies, *A Midsummer Night's Dream* resembles a fertility rite, for the sterile world that Titania depicts at the beginning of act 2 is trans-

Shirley Nelson Garner, "*A Midsummer Night's Dream*: 'Jack shall have Jill; / Nought shall go ill,'" *Women's Studies: An Inter-Disciplinary Journal*, 1966, pp. 47–63. Copyright © 1966 by Taylor & Francis Group. All rights reserved. Reproduced by permission.

formed and the play concludes with high celebration, ritual blessing, and the promise of regeneration.[2] Though this pattern is easily apparent and has often been observed, the social and sexual implications of the return of the green world have gone unnoticed. What has not been so clearly seen is that the renewal at the end of the play affirms patriarchal order and hierarchy, insisting that the power of women must be circumscribed, and that it recognizes the tenuousness of heterosexuality as well.[3] The movement of the play toward ordering the fairy, human, and natural worlds is also a movement toward satisfying men's psychological needs, as Shakespeare perceived them, but its cost is the disruption of women's bonds with each other.

I

Regeneration finally depends on the amity between Titania and Oberon. As she tells him, their quarrel over possession of an Indian boy has brought chaos, disease, and sterility to the natural world:

> And this same progeny of evils comes
>
> From our debate, from our dissension;
>
> We are their parents and original.
>
> (II.i.115–17)

The story of the "lovely boy" is told from two points of view, Puck's and Titania's. Puck tells a companion fairy that Oberon is "passing fell and wrath" because Titania has taken as her attendant "a lovely boy, stolen from an Indian king"; he continues:

> She never had so sweet a changeling.
>
> And jealous Oberon would have the child
>
> Knight of his train, to trace the forests wild.
>
> But she perforce withholds the lovéd boy,

> Crowns him with flowers, and makes him all her joy.
>
> And now they never meet in grove or green,
>
> By fountain dear, or spangled starlight sheen,
>
> But they do square, that all the elves for fear
>
> Creep into acorn cups and hide them there.
>
> (II.i.18–31)

Shortly afterward, when Oberon tells Titania that it is up to her to amend their quarrel and that he merely begs "a little changeling boy" to be his "henchman," she retorts, "Set your heart at rest. / The fairy land buys not the child of me." Then she explains the child's origin, arguing her loyalty to the child's mother to be the reason for keeping him:

> His mother was a vot'ress of my order,
>
> And, in the spicèd Indian air, by night,
>
> Full often hath she gossiped by my side,
>
> And sat with me on Neptune's yellow sands,
>
> Marking th' embarkèd traders on the flood;
>
> When we have laughed to see the sails conceive
>
> And grow big-bellied with the wanton wind;
>
> Which she, with pretty and with swimming gait
>
> Following—her womb then rich with my young squire—
>
> Would imitate, and sail upon the land,
>
> To fetch me trifles, and return again,
>
> As from a voyage, rich with merchandise.

But she, being mortal, of that boy did die;

And for her sake do I rear up her boy,

And for her sake I will not part with him.

(II.i.121–37)

Both accounts affirm that the child has become the object of Titania's love, but the shift in emphasis from one point of view to the other is significant. Puck describes the child as "stolen from an Indian king," whereas Titania emphasizes the child's link with his mother, her votaress. Puck's perspective, undoubtedly close to Oberon's, ignores or suppresses the connection between Titania and the Indian queen, which, in its exclusion of men and suggestion of love between women, threatens patriarchal and heterosexual values.[4]

Titania's attachment to the boy is clearly erotic. She "crowns him with flowers, and makes him all her joy," according him the same attentions as those she bestows on Bottom when, under the spell of Oberon's love potion, she falls in love with the rustic turned ass. She has "forsworn" Oberon's "bed and company" (II.i.62). Whatever the child is to her as a "lovely boy" and a "sweet" changeling, he is ultimately her link with a mortal woman whom she loved. Oberon's passionate determination to have the child for himself suggests that he is both attracted to and jealous of him. He would have not only the boy but also the exclusive love of Titania.[5] He needs to cut her off from the child because she is attracted to him not only as boy and child, but also as his mother's son. Oberon's need to humiliate Titania in attaining the boy suggests that her love for the child poses a severe threat to the fairy king.

Puck's statement that Oberon wants the child to be "knight of his train" and Oberon's that he wants him to be his "henchman" have led some critics to argue that the fairy king's desires to have the boy are more appropriate than the fairy queen's. Oberon's wish to have the boy is consistent with the practice of taking boys from the nursery to the father's realm so that they can acquire the character and skills appropriate to manhood.⁶ But Puck describes Oberon as "jealous," and his emphasis on the "lovely boy," the "sweet" changeling, and the "lovéd boy" (II.ii.20–7) suggests that Oberon, like Titania, is attracted to the child. There is no suggestion that Oberon wants to groom the child for manhood; he wants him rather "to trace the forests wild" (1.25) with his fairy band. Those critics who attribute moral intentions to Oberon, arguing for his benevolent motives in taking the boy from Titania, overlook that Oberon has no intention of returning him to his father, with whom he, as a human child, might be most properly reared. When we last hear of the boy, Titania's fairy has carried him to Oberon's "bower" (IV.i.62).

Oberon's winning the boy from Titania is at the center of the play, for his victory is the price of amity between them, which in turn restores the green world. At the beginning, Oberon and Titania would seem to have equal magical powers, but Oberon's power proves the greater. Since he cannot persuade Titania to turn over the boy to him, he humiliates her and torments her until she does so. He uses the love potion not simply to divert her attention from the child, so that he can have him, but to punish her as well.⁷ As he squeezes the love flower on Titania's eyes, he speaks a charm—or rather a curse—revealing his intention:

What thou see'st when thou dost wake,

Do it for thy truelove take;

Love and languish for his sake.

Be it ounce, or cat, or bear,

Pard, or boar with bristled hair,

In thy eye that shall appear

When thou wak'st, it is thy dear.

Wake when some vile thing is near.

(II.ii.27–34)

When Puck tells him that Titania is "with a monster in love" (III.ii.6), he is obviously pleased: "This falls out better than I could devise" (1.35).

Though the scenes between Titania and Bottom are charming and hilarious, Titania is made ridiculous. Whereas her opening speech is remarkable for its lyric beauty, and her defense of keeping the Indian boy has quiet and dignified emotional power, now she is reduced to admiring Bottom's truisms and his monstrous shape: "Thou art as wise as thou art beautiful" (III.i.147). However enjoyable the scenes between her and Bottom, however thematically satisfying in their representation of the marriage of our animal and spiritual natures, Titania, free of the influence of Oberon's love potion, says of Bottom, "O, how mine eyes do loathe his visage now!" (V.i.80). By his own account, Oberon taunts Titania into obedience; he tells Puck:

See'st thou this sweet sight?

Her dotage now I do begin to pity:

For, meeting her of late behind the wood,

Seeking sweet favors for this hateful fool,

I did upbraid her, and fall out with her.

For she his hairy temples then had rounded

With coronet of fresh and fragrant flowers;

And that same dew, which sometime on the buds

Was wont to swell, like round and orient pearls,

Stood now within the pretty flouriet's eyes,

> Like tears, that did their own disgrace bewail.
>
> When I had at my pleasure taunted her,
>
> And she in mild terms begged my patience,
>
> I then did ask of her her changeling child;
>
> Which straight she gave me, and her fairy sent
>
> To bear him to my bower in fairy land.
>
> And now I have the boy, I will undo
>
> This hateful imperfection of her eyes.
>
> (IV.i.47–64)

Oberon gains the exclusive love of Titania and also possession of the boy to whom he is attracted. But his gain is Titania's loss: she is separated from the boy and, in that separation, further severed from the woman whom she had loved. Oberon can offer ritual blessing at the play's end because he has what he wanted from the beginning: Titania obedient and under his control and the beautiful Indian boy in his bower.

II

Like the fairy king, the two men in power in the human world, Theseus and Egeus, want to attain the exclusive love of a woman and, also, to accommodate their homoerotic desires.[8] In order to do so, they, like Oberon, attempt to limit women's power, and their success or failure to do so affects their participation in the comic world.

The opening of *A Midsummer Night's Dream* puts Hippolyta's subjugation in bold relief as Theseus reminds his bride-to-be:

> Hippolyta, I wooed thee with my sword,
>
> And won thy love, doing thee injuries;

But I will wed thee in another key,

With pomp, with triumph, and with reveling.

(I.i.16–19)

Capturing Hippolyta when he defeated the Amazons, Theseus has abducted her from her Amazon sisters to bring her to Athens and marry her. Though most directors play Hippolyta as a willing bride, I once saw San Francisco's Actor's Workshop, following the cues of Jan Kott, bring her on stage clothed in skins and imprisoned in a cage.[9] The text invites such a rendering, for almost immediately it sets her apart from Theseus by implying that she sides with Hermia and Lysander against Egeus and Theseus, when he sanctions Egeus's authority. After Theseus tells Hermia to prepare to marry Demetrius or "on Diana's altar to protest / For aye austerity and single life" (I.i.89–90) and then beckons Hippolyta to follow him offstage, he undoubtedly notices her frowning, for he asks, "What cheer, my love?" (I.i.122). Shakespeare heightens her isolation by presenting her without any Amazon attendants.

Though Theseus is less severe than Egeus, he is, from the outset, unsympathetic toward women. The first words he speaks, voicing the play's first lines and first image, must be taken as a sign: the moon "lingers" his desires, he tells Hippolyta, "Like a stepdame, or a dowager, / Long withering out a young man's revenue." He utterly supports Egeus as patriarch, telling Hermia:

To you your father should be as a god,

One that composed your beauties; yea, and one

To whom you are but as a form in wax

By him imprinted and within his power

To leave the figure or disfigure it.

(I.i.47–51)

As a ruler, he will enforce the law, which gives Egeus control over Hermia's sexuality and embodies patriarchal order. Though he has heard that Demetrius has won Helena's heart but now scorns her, and has meant to speak to him about it, "My mind did lose it" (I.i.114). A lover-and-leaver of women himself, he undoubtedly identifies with Demetrius and forgets his duty toward Helena. He exits inviting Egeus and Demetrius to follow and talk confidentially with him, suggesting his spiritual kinship with them.

Whatever other associations Theseus had for Shakespeare's audience, he was notorious as the first seducer of Helen.[10] As early as act II, Oberon recalls Theseus's reputation as a deserter of women.[11] When Titania accuses Oberon of infidelity, asking rhetorically why he was in Athens if not to see Hippolyta, "the bouncing Amazon, / Your buskined mistress and your warrior love"(II.i.70–71), he accuses her of loving Theseus:

> Didst not thou lead him through the glimmering night
>
> From Perigenia, whom he ravished?
>
> And make him with fair Aegles break his faith,
>
> With Ariadne and Antiopa?
>
> (II.77–80)

It is significant that the woman whom he at last will marry is not traditionally feminine. She has been a warrior, and in her new role as the fiancée of the Athenian duke, we see her as a hunter. Nostalgically, she recalls her past experiences:

> I was with Hercules and Cadmus once,
>
> When in a wood of Crete they bayed the bear
>
> With hounds of Sparta. Never did I hear

Such gallant chiding; for, besides the groves,

The skies, the fountains, every region near

Seemed all one mutual cry. I never heard

So musical a discord, such sweet thunder.

(IV.i.113–119)

Her androgynous character appears to resolve for Theseus the apparent dissociation of his romantic life, the sign of which is his continual desertion of women who love him.[12]

Having found an androgynous woman, Theseus captures her and brings her home to be his wife. By conquering and marrying this extraordinarily powerful woman, he fulfills his need for the exclusive love of a woman while gratifying his homoerotic desires.[13] Unlike Oberon, however, he finds satisfaction for his desires merged in one person. If we imagine Hippolyta played by a male actor who, though cast as a woman, dresses and walks like a man ("buskined mistress," "bouncing Amazon"), Hippolyta and Theseus must have looked more like homosexual than heterosexual lovers. Hippolyta's androgynous appearance is further confirmed by the fact that in Renaissance fiction and drama men were occasionally disguised as Amazons, e.g., lovers, like Sidney's Zelmane, in *Arcadia*, who wished to be near his lady.[14] Hippolyta, like Viola and Rosalind in disguise, fulfills a male fantasy, and more happily so since she is not in disguise. Because Theseus's romantic life is fortunately resolved once the young lovers have paired themselves off anew, with Demetrius loving Helena, he can sanction their preferences and ignore Egeus's persistent demand that Hermia marry Demetrius.[15]

By insisting that Hermia marry Demetrius, Egeus hopes to keep his daughter rather than lose her and to have Demetrius near him as well. Shakespeare makes Egeus's motives suspect by creating him foolishly comic, treating him more harshly than he does his other controlling and possessive fathers—

Lear, Capulet, Brabantio, Shylock, Prospero. Unable to make his daughter marry where he wishes, Egeus turns to the law to enforce his will. More outrageous than Brabantio, he turns Lysander's courtship of his daughter into a series of crimes: Lysander has "bewitched the bosom" of Hermia, "stol'n the impression of her fantasy," "filched" her heart (I.i.26–38). As Shakespeare depicts the two lovers who compete over Hermia, he is careful to draw them so that Egeus's choice is irrational and not in Hermia's best interests. Lysander states his case before Theseus:

> I am, my lord, as well derived as he [Demetrius],
>
> As well possessed; my love is more than his;
>
> My fortunes every way as fairly ranked
>
> (If not with vantage) as Demetrius';
>
> And, which is more than all these boasts can be,
>
> I am beloved of beauteous Hermia.
>
> (I.i.99–104)

Lysander continues to accuse Demetrius of making love to Helena, who now "dotes in idolatry, / Upon this spotted and inconstant man" (II.109–110). His accusation is evidently founded, for Theseus confesses that he has "heard so much" (I.111) and Demetrius does not deny it or defend himself. Later, Demetrius admits that he was betrothed to Helena before he saw Hermia (IV.i.172–73). Egeus chooses badly for his daughter unless he wishes to keep her for himself, as I think he does. By insisting that she marry a man whom she does not love and one who may be unfaithful to her besides, if his present conduct is a gauge, Egeus assures that she will always love her father; that she will never really leave him.

There are suggestions, as well, that Egeus has a particular affection for Demetrius. Shakespeare does not leave us to assume that Egeus's preference for Demetrius is simply proprietary, i.e., since Hermia is his, he may give her as he chooses; or that it is simply an affirmation of male bonding, like Capulet's demand that Juliet marry Paris, "And you be mine, I'll give you to my friend" (*Rom.* III.v.193). Lysander's sarcasm defines Egeus's feeling for Demetrius:

> You have her father's love, Demetrius;
>
> Let me have Hermia's: do you marry him.
>
> (I.i.93–94)

And Egeus immediately affirms:

> True, he hath my love,
>
> And what is mine, my love shall render him.

Even after Demetrius has fallen in love with Helena, Egeus continues to pair himself with him. When the lovers are discovered asleep in the forest coupled "right" at last and Lysander begins to explain what Theseus calls their "gentle concord," Egeus urges:

> Enough, enough, my lord; you have enough.
>
> I beg the law, the law, upon his head.
>
> They would have stol'n away; they would, Demetrius,
>
> Thereby to have defeated you and me,
>
> You of your wife and me of my consent,
>
> Of my consent that she should be your wife.
>
> (IV.i.55–60)

Egeus would draw Demetrius back to him, realigning the original *we* against *them*.

The quarrel between Oberon and Titania began over the Indian boy in Titania's care. Titania tells Oberon that their quarrelling has upset nature. Oberon vows to punish Titania for her disobedience and comes up with a plan to humiliate her, treating her not as an equal but as an object he can control. © Sir Joseph Noel Paton/The Bridgeman Art Library/Getty Images.

Egeus, then, has hoped to have the exclusive love of Hermia and to accommodate his homoerotic feelings by binding Demetrius to him. To give up Hermia and accept that Demetrius loves Helena would defeat him doubly. Consequently, he leaves the stage unreconciled. Had it been left to him to affirm the comic resolution, we would have none.

III

Whereas the separation of Hippolyta and Titania from other women is implied or kept in the background, the breaking of women's bonds is central in the plot involving the four young lovers.[16] Demetrius and Lysander are divided at the outset, but the play dramatizes the division of Hermia and Helena. Furthermore, their quarreling is more demeaning than the men's. And once Demetrius and Lysander are no longer in competition for the same woman, their enmity is gone. Hermia and Helena, on the contrary, seem permanently separated and apparently give over their power to the men they will marry. Once their friendship is undermined and their power diminished, they are presumably "ready" for marriage.

Hermia's fond recollection of her long-standing and intimate friendship with Helena calls attention to Helena's disloyalty, occasioned by the latter's desire to win Demetrius's thanks and to be near him. Telling her friend that she intends to run away with Lysander, Hermia recalls:

> And in the wood, where often you and I
>
> Upon faint primrose beds were wont to lie,
>
> Emptying our bosoms of their counsel sweet,
>
> There my Lysander and myself shall meet.
>
> (I.i.214–217)

Just as Helena breaks her faith with Hermia to ingratiate herself with Demetrius, so later she will believe that Hermia has joined with men against her. Deeply hurt, Helena chastises Hermia:

> Is all the counsel that we two have shared,
>
> The sister's vows, the hours that we have spent,
>
> When we have chid the hasty-footed time
>
> For parting us—O, is all forgot?
>
> All school-days' friendship, childhood innocence?
>
> We, Hermia, like two artificial gods,
>
> Have with our needles created both one flower,
>
> Both on one sampler, sitting on one cushion,

> Both warbling of one song, both in one key;
>
> As if our hands, our sides, voices, and minds,
>
> Had been incorporate. So we grew together,
>
> Like to a double cherry, seeming parted
>
> But yet an union in partition,
>
> Two lovely berries molded on one stem;
>
> So, with two seeming bodies, but one heart;
>
> Two of the first, like coats in heraldry,
>
> Due but to one, and crowned with one crest.
>
> And will you rent our ancient love asunder,
>
> To join with men in scorning your poor friend?
>
> It is not friendly, 'tis not maidenly.
>
> Our sex, as well as I, may chide you for it,
>
> Though I alone do feel the injury.
>
> (III.ii.198–219)

In a scene that parallels in its central position Titania's wooing of Bottom, the rupture of their friendship becomes final. They accuse and insult each other, with Hermia calling Helena a "juggler," "canker blossom," "thief of love," "painted maypole"; and Helena naming her a "counterfeit" and a "puppet" (III.ii.282–296). Their quarrel becomes absurd as it turns on Hermia's obsession, taken up by both Lysander and Helena, that Lysander has come to prefer Helena because she is taller. Though no other women characters in Shakespeare's plays come close to fighting physically, Hermia threatens to scratch out Helena's eyes (III.ii.297–98). Her threat is serious enough to make Helena flee (II.340–43). Lysander is made equally ridiculous in his abrupt change of heart; yet he and Demetrius are spared the indignity of a demeaning quarrel and leave the stage to settle their disagreement in a "manly" fashion, with swords. Even though Puck makes a mockery of their combat through his teasing, they are not so thoroughly diminished as Hermia and Helena.

In the course of the play, both Hermia and Helena suffer at the hands of their lovers. Betrothed to Helena, Demetrius deserts her for Hermia. When she pursues him, he tells her that she makes him sick (II.i.212) and threatens to rape her (II.214–219). By doggedly following him, she maintains a kind of desperate power over him. She will not play Dido to his Aeneas. Consequently, he cannot sustain the image of the romantic rake, whose women pine and die, commit suicide, or burn themselves on pyres when he leaves them. Disappointed in his love for Hermia, he cannot get loose from Helena. Yet her masochism undercuts her power:

I am your spaniel; and, Demetrius,

The more you beat me, I will fawn on you.

Use me but as your spaniel, spurn me, strike me,

Neglect me, lose me; only give me leave,

Unworthy as I am, to follow you.

What worser place can I beg in your love—

And yet a place of high respect with me—

Than to be usèd as you use your dog?

(II.i.202–210)

When Helena is in a position of positive power with both Lysander and Demetrius in love with her, she cannot take advantage of it because she assumes that she is the butt of a joke. And of course, in a sense, she is right: she is the victim of either Puck's prank or his mistake. Hermia must also bear Lysander's contempt. In the forest, he insists that he "hates" her (III.ii.270, 281) and calls her outrageous names: "cat," "burr," "vile thing," "tawny Tartar," "loathed med'cine," "hated potion," "dwarf," "minimus, of hind'ring knotgrass made," "bead," "acorn," (II.260–64, 328–330). While both women protest their lovers' treatment of them, neither can play Beatrice to her Benedick. Both more or less bear their lovers' abuses.

After the four lovers sleep and awaken coupled as they will marry, Hermia and Helena do not reconcile. Once they leave the forest, they lose their voices. Neither of them speaks again. Recognizing that it is difficult for an actor to be on stage without any lines, as Helena and Hermia are for almost all of act 5, Shakespeare was undoubtedly aware that he was creating a portentous silence. Since Helena and Hermia are evidently married between acts 4 and 5, their silence suggests that in their new roles as wives they will be obedient, allowing their husbands dominance.

IV

The end of *A Midsummer Night's Dream* is as fully joyous as the conclusion of any of Shakespeare's comedies. No longer angry with each other, Oberon and Titania bring blessing to the human world:

> Hand in hand, with fairy grace,
> Will we sing, and bless this place.
> (V.i.398–99)

Though Oberon calls up dark possibilities, he offers a charm against them. The prospect of love, peace, safety, prosperity is as promising as it ever will be. The cost of this harmony, however, is the restoration of patriarchal hierarchy, so threatened at the beginning of the play. This return to the old order depends on the breaking of women's bonds with each other and the submission of women, which the play relentlessly exacts. Puck's verse provides the paradigm:

> Jack shall have Jill;
>
> Nought shall go ill;
>
> The man shall have his mare again,
>
> and all shall be well.

If we turn to some of Shakespeare's comedies in which women's bonds with each other are unbroken and their power is left intact or even dominates, the tone of the ending is less harmonious or even discordant.[17] In *The Merchant of Venice*, for example, where Portia is in control and she and Nerissa triumph over Gratiano and Bassanio, there is no ritual celebration. Portia directs the scene and carefully circumscribes her marriage with Bassanio to close out Antonio. When she and Nerissa reveal their identities as the doctor and the clerk, they make clear their extraordinary power to outwit and deceive, calling up women's ultimate destructive power in marriage and love—to cuckold. The final moments of the play move toward reconciliation, but not celebration. The last line, a bawdy joke, is spoken by Gratiano, the most hate-filled character in the play, and reminds us of men's fear of women and their need to control them: "While I live I'll fear no other thing / So sore, as keeping safe Nerissa's ring" (V.i.306–307).

In *Love's Labour's Lost*, where the women remain together and in control, there is no comic ending.[18] Echoing Puck, Berowne makes the point as he speaks to the King of Navarre:

> Our wooing doth not end like an old play;
>
> Jack hath not Jill. These ladies' courtesy
>
> Might well have made our sport a comedy.

When the King replies, "Come, sir, it wants a twelvemonth and a day, / And then 'twill end," Berowne answers, "That's too long for a play" (V.ii.872–76). The refrains of the closing songs call forth images of cuckolding and of "greasy Joan" stirring the pot.

The pattern of these comic endings suggest that heterosexual bonding is tenuous at best. In order to be secure, to enjoy, to love—to participate in the celebration that comedy invites—men need to maintain their ties with other men and to sever women's bonds with each other. The implication is that men fear that if women join with each other, they will not need men, will possibly exclude them or prefer the friendship and love of women. This is precisely the threat of the beautiful scene that Titania describes between herself and her votaress. This fear may be based partially on reality, but it is also partially caused by projection: Since men have traditionally had stronger bonds with other men than with women and have excluded women from participation in things about which they cared most, they may assume that women, granted the opportunity, will do the same. Given this possibility or likelihood, Shakespeare's male characters act out of a fear of women's bonding with each other and a feeling of sexual powerlessness. The male characters think they can keep their women only if they divide and conquer them. Only then will Jack have Jill; only then will their world flourish.

Notes

1. William Shakespeare, *The Complete Signet Classic Shakespeare*, ed., Sylvan Barnet (New York: Harcourt, 1972), *MND*, III.ii.461–64. Subsequent quotations from Shakespeare are from this edition.
2. C.L. Barber, *Shakespeare's Festive Comedy: A Study of Dramatic Form and Its Relation to Social Custom*, 2nd ed. (1959; rpt. Cleveland, Ohio: World, 1963), pp. 119–124, 127.
3. In "Hermia's Dream: Royal Road to *A Midsummer Night's Dream*" (*Literature and Psychology*, 22 [1972], 188–89), M.D. Faber has observed that "the order for which the play strives is a severely patriarchal one which, by its very nature, engenders ambivalence and hostility in women and thus produces a constant straining toward disorder." Yet Faber's insistences that Theseus, "a governor of strength and understanding," has transcended rigid patriarchal attitudes and his suggestion that women are responsible for disorder make clear that our arguments are substantially different.
4. Describing Titania's lines are "one of the most beautiful bravura speeches," Barber remarks that the moment is "a glimpse of women who gossip alone, apart from men and feeling now no need of them, rejoicing in their own special part of life' power" (pp. 136–37).
5. Some male critics regard Titania's love as Oberon's right; Melvin Goldstein writes: "We know also that Titania violates natural order by making the changeling

child 'all her joy', when all her joy should be Oberon" ("Identity Crises in a Midsummer Nightmare: Comedy as Terror in Disguise," *Psychoanalytic Review*, 60 [1973], 189).

6. Goldstein argues, for example, that Titania "needs to give up the boy not only for Oberon's and for her sake, but for the boy's sake. The danger is that in her company and that of her women friends she will feminize him" (p. 18). In his introduction to the new Arden edition of *A Midsummer Night's Dream* (London: Methuen, 1979), Harold F. Brooks states, "It is perhaps (Puck may imply this) high time the boy was weaned from maternal dandling to be bred a knight and huntsman" (p. cvi).

7. Jan Kott, *Shakespeare Our Contemporary*, trans., Boleslaw Taborski (Garden City, New York: Doubleday, 1966), p. 227.

8. I use "homoerotic desires" to mean unconsummated homosexual feeling, which may or may not be recognized.

9. Allan Lewis describes John Hancock's even more extreme presentation of Hippolyta in his production of the play in Greenwich Village in 1967: she was "brought back in captivity, robed in leopard skins, was caged and guarded" ("A Midsummer Night's Dream—Fairy Fantasy or Erotic Nightmare?," *Educational Theatre Journal*, 21 [1969], 251).

10. References to Theseus and Helen are commonplace in the Renaissance. George Gascoigne, who uses the most ordinary classical allusions, addresses Paris in "Dan Bartholmew His First Triumpe," one of the poems from *Dan Bartholmew of Bathe*:

"Alas, shee made of thee, a noddye for the nonce,

For Menelaus lost hir twise, though thou hir foundst but once.

But yet if in thine eye, shee seemde a peerelesse peece,

Aske Theseus the mighty Duke, what towns she knew in Greece?

Aske him what made hir leave hir wofull aged sire,

And steale to Athens gyglot like: what? what but foule desire?"

(*The Posies*, ed., John W. Cunliffe [Cambridge: Cambridge Univ. Press, [1907], I.101).

11. In an excellent article, "'Unkinde' Theseus: A Study in Renaissance Mythography" (*ELR*, 4 [1973], 276–98), D'Orsay W. Pearson outlines classical and Renaissance traditions that depict Theseus's darker side, particularly his treacherous and abusive treatment of women. Shakespeare's audience would have been familiar with these traditions. If in remembering Theseus's heroic exploits, they forgot his "unkindness," Shakespeare was careful to remind them by recalling women Theseus had loved and left. Pearson also analyzes Theseus's opening speech, describing ways in which it suggests his negative Renaissance stereotype (p. 292).

12. In his frequent desertion of women, Theseus acts similarly to men Freud describes as evincing a dissociated erotic life. See "A Special Type of Choice of Object Made by Men" and "On the Universal Tendency to Debasement in the Sphere of Love," *The Standard Edition of the Complete Psychological Works of Sigmund Freud*, trans., James Strachey (London: Hogarth, 1957), XI, 166–67, 182–83.

13. In "The Sexual Aberrations," the first of his *Three Contributions on the Theory of Sex*, Freud comments that a large proportion of male homosexuals "retain the mental quality of masculinity ... and that what they look for in the real sexual object are in fact feminine mental traits." Their "sexual object is not someone of the same sex, but someone who combines the characters of both sexes ... a union of

both sex characteristics, a compromise between an impulse that seeks for a man and one that seeks for a woman" (VII, 144–45).

14. Celeste Turner Wright, "The Amazons in Elizabethan Literature," (*SP*, 37 [1940], 439).

15. E.K. Chambers notices that Theseus's marriage to Hippolyta evinces a change in character: "Theseus has had his wayward youth;... moreover, in his passion for Hippolyta he has approached her through deeds of violence; he has 'won her love, doing her injuries.' But now, like Henry the Fifth of whom he is the prototype, he has put away childish things; he stands forth as the serene law-abiding king, no less than the still loving and tender husband" (*Shakespeare: A Survey* [London: Sidgwick and Jackson, 1925], pp. 84–85. Chambers is right in observing that Theseus has changed. I suggest that the change is not one of character but as a result of altered situation; i.e., he has captured a woman who at last can fulfill his romantic needs, which until now have been disparate.

16. In considering the modification Shakespeare made in his construction of the plot involving the Athenian lovers, Chambers points especially to his "making the broken friendship that of women, not that of men" (p. 82). In Chaucer's *Knight's Tale*, which Shakespeare drew on, Palomon's and Arcite's common love of Emilia breaks their friendship. In *The Two Gentleman of Verona*, in which the relation of Proteus and Valentine corresponds to that of Palomon and Arcite, the friendship between the two men is disrupted though two women, rather than one, are involved. Shakespeare's alteration of Chaucer's tale and variation of his former pattern in *A Midsummer Night's Dream* suggest that the disruption of women's bonds was a significant theme.

17. In a fine essay, "Sexual Politics and the Social Structure in *As You Like It*," Peter B. Erickson has argued similarly in comparing the endings of *As You Like It* and *Love's Labour's Lost*: "The ending of *As You Like It* works smoothly because male control is affirmed and women are rendered nonthreatening, whereas in *Love's Labour's Lost* women do not surrender their independence and the status of patriarchal, social order is securely in place" (unpublished paper delivered at the session on "Marriage and the Family in Shakespeare," sponsored by the Shakespeare Division, at the annual meeting of the MLA, 1979; pp. 3, 15; forthcoming in the *Massachusetts Review*).

18. See Peter Erickson, "The Failure of Relationship Between Men and Women in *Love's Labour's Lost*," this issue, *Women's Studies*.

Productions of *A Midsummer Night's Dream* Have Evolved Over the Years

W. Reginald Rampone Jr.

W. Reginald Rampone Jr. *teaches at South Carolina State University. He is an expert on English Renaissance literature.*

Rampone surveys performances of A Midsummer Night's Dream *from Shakespeare's time up until the present. In the early years, directors often shortened the play to suit their own production needs. In the nineteenth century, bringing out the spectacle of the play was favored over historical and textual accuracy. It was in the twentieth century, Rampone writes, that sexuality became a major force in stage and screen productions. Influenced by the writings of critic Jan Kott, director Peter Brook highlighted the sexual nature of the plot. Since then, productions of* A Midsummer Night's Dream *have focused more and more on its sexual conflicts, investigating both traditional and alternative sexualities. Harking back to the original productions of the play, some modern-day versions have used an all-male cast, and given the current interest in early theatrical practices, Rampone predicts that more single-sex versions of the play will be produced.*

Although *A Midsummer Night's Dream* was written in 1595 or 1596, the exact date of its performance cannot be established. Like many of Shakespeare's plays, *A Midsummer Night's Dream* also underwent textual changes. Between 1661 and 1816 *A Midsummer Night's Dream* underwent a number of truncations and abbreviations. In 1662 [English diarist]

W. Reginald Rampone Jr., *Sexuality in the Age of Shakespeare*, 2011, pp. 89–95. Copyright © ABC-CLIO. All rights reserved. Reproduced by permission.

Samuel Pepys, an inveterate playgoer, attended a performance of *A Midsummer Night's Dream*, and he later wrote in his diary that it was the most absurd play that he had ever seen.

Nineteenth-Century Productions

Not only did directors and actors significantly change the play by shortening it in order to suit their own dramatic needs, but they were also bothered by its plot. When Francis Gentleman edited the text in 1774 for *[Bell's Edition of Shakespeare's Plays]*, he was concerned about its childish plot with a miscellany of events and contrived arrangements of different styles. Edward Malone, another very important editor of the period, was infuriated to find the "fable thus meager and uninteresting".

By 1816, the theatre manager Madame Lucia Elizabeth Vestris and an Italian contralto began to restore Shakespeare's text to the play in Vestris's production of it in Covent Garden in 1840. Actually, James Robinson Planché deserves a great deal of the credit for restoring Shakespeare's language to the play; he was also responsible for the costumes and the beautiful last scene, which was extraordinary with more than 50 fairies flying or dancing around the galleries and stairs. In fact, Vestris played the queen of the fairies, Titania, and sang nine songs while a girl played the role of Puck.

The next great shift in *A Midsummer Night's Dream* occurred on October 15, 1856, in Charles Kean's production in which he deleted 800 lines in order for the performance to last less than three hours in spite of all of the dancing and [Felix] Mendelssohn's music. By the end of the 19th century, Augustin Daly had gone to even greater lengths in his creation of spectacles and pantomimes in 1873, and later in 1888 he staged the play with [actors] John Drew, Otis Skinner, and Ada Rehan while [American dancer] Isadora Duncan went so far as to wear papier-mâché wings. By 1895 Daly had placed electrical lights on his fairies, and Lillian Swain played the role of Puck and Ada Rehan played the role of Oberon, receiving high praise from [Irish playwright] George Bernard Shaw.

Spectacle Over Historical Accuracy

Increasingly, spectacle was touted over historical and textual accuracy by [British actor] Herbert Beerbohm Tree, whose 1900 production of *A Midsummer Night's Dream* was a vision of pictorial splendor with thyme and wild flowers and thickets and a background of trees replete with rabbits running across the stage as Julia Neilson played Oberon. Other directors who lacked the financial resources of Tree, such as William Poel, Gordon Craig, and Harley Granville-Barker, had other ideas regarding the staging of Shakespeare's plays by reducing the amount of scenery and thereby reducing the visual distractions. While some 220,000 people saw Tree's production of *A Midsummer Night's Dream*, the advent of film would increase a director's audience to an unprecedented number of viewers.

Max Reinhardt also celebrated the magnificence of pictorialism. He had begun directing *A Midsummer Night's Dream* in 1905 at Neues Theatre in Berlin and continued to direct it all over Europe eventually reaching Los Angeles's Hollywood Bowl in 1934, and finally, it culminated in his celebrated film version of 1935 with American actors Mickey Rooney as Puck, James Cagney as [Nick] Bottom, Anita Louise as Titania, Victor Jory as Oberon, Olivia de Havilland as Hermia, and Dick Powell as Lysander, all of whom were big-name Hollywood stars. This magnificent production cost Warner Brothers $1.5 million and used a sound stage of over 38,000 feet. [Austro-Hungarian composer] Erich Wolfgang Korngold arranged the music according to Mendelssohn's *Overture to a Midsummer Night's Dream* in addition to incidental music.

Despite the joy of young love and marriage, there is clearly an undercurrent of evil in the [William] Dieterle–[Max] Reinhardt version of this film. [Kenneth] Rothwell rightly remarks upon this film's "darker gothic subtext, embodying in its varied strings and horns the contradictory motifs to come—nuptials and feasting, and high hopes, yet poised on the edge of a dark wood harboring acts of unspeakable bestiality." Others have noted the untoward edginess that lurks beneath the surface of the filmic text; [critic] Philip McGuire notes Hippolyta's silence at the beginning of the film. He suggests that she is angry at the rape of the Amazons, and so she may have a feminist agenda. [Critic Jay] Halio believes that it is best that Titania and Bottom's erotic encounter not be discussed because it is so absurd, but it is heartfelt and emotionally engaging. When Oberon sees his fairy queen, he begins to have pity on her and, finally, removes the spell. Meanwhile, the gnome orchestra performs Mendelssohn's "Nocturne."

Modern Film Versions and Sexuality

The next version of *A Midsummer Night's Dream* of import is Peter Hall's 1968 film version in which Derek Godfrey played Theseus, Ian Holm played Puck, Judi Dench played Titania, and Helen Mirren played Hermia. This film version, like Max Reinhardt's, presents the dark side of human existence. Rothwell suggests that Hall "stabs at the darker side of the dream, the dream that turns into a nightmare in a dark wood." The eroticism in this film is quite palpable as Titania and Oberon are virtually nude. Titania wears what looks like a bikini bottom and nothing covering her breasts; Oberon appears as a satyr with pointed ears and a green complexion, and Oberon's behavior is completely in keeping with his appearance, yet despite the sinister quality about Reinhardt's Oberon, Hall decided to focus upon the sensuality of their sexual relations and not its brutality; after all, the spell under which Oberon places Titania allows her to fall in love with any wild animal, and it could prove to be physically and emotionally devastating to her. When Titania does become enamored of Bottom, she does not allow him to escape her, but he reluctantly agrees to go to her bower. Then she lowers him to the ground in order to engage in sexual intercourse.

Rehearsals for Peter Brook's groundbreaking version of *A Midsummer Night's Dream* began in the summer of 1970 and continued for eight weeks until the production began. Brook was concerned with the actors conforming to his concept of the production. The set was to resemble a white squash court which had two small stage doors in the rear wall with ladders on the downstage edges which would lead to catwalks. From these galleries the actors could watch the play when they were not onstage. Titania's bower was a hammock made of red ostrich feathers, and the fairies had trapezes to use as needed, and the actors wore oversized pants that were loose and baggy, made of satin and tie-dyed blouses, and the women wore dresses that were like tunics. The fairies wore plain tunics, except for Oberon, Titania, and Puck, who wore bright colors that were fluorescent, which created a strong contrast against the white walls of the set. Oberon and Titania wore silk gowns while Puck had an oversized jumpsuit. Brook also decided to double the actors' roles by having Theseus and Hippolyta play the roles of Oberon and Titania respectively. Brook may well have implied that Oberon and Titania were the alter egos of Theseus and Hippolyta by having them double up these roles. Finally, the set was extremely well lighted as Brook believed that it was necessary to dispel any sense of illusion about the play. As provocative as this production was scenically, the actors' amorphous costumes certainly did not eroticize the characters' bodies.

By dispelling any sense of illusion, Brook could address issues of sexuality. He very much wanted to emphasize the relationship of love and sexuality or rather love in its relation to sexuality. It was at this time that Brook had formed a significant friendship with Jan Kott, who was an important Polish scholar and critic, and whose book *Shakespeare Our Contemporary* was very influential to Brook in his understanding of both [Shakespeare's tragedy] *King Lear* and *A Midsummer Night's Dream*. Kott argued that much criticism and performances of this play failed to recognize the play's very powerful sense of sexuality and violence. Halio in the same vein argues that the fact that Theseus wooed Hippolyta with violence presages the violation that Oberon enacts when he places the love juice on Titania's eyes later in the play in addition to the rancor that ensues once the lovers enter the woods. The fact that Titania wooed an ass is of particular significance. Kott says that all of the animals that Oberon mentions while conjuring his spell are those of great sexual potency, but of all the animals that he mentions, the ass is the one that has the greatest sexual power and the largest and hardest penis. Moreover, Titania engages with the unsavory sphere of sexuality with much greater intensity than any other character in the play. The interaction between them continues to intrigue audience members.

The sexual intensity between the young lovers is also made manifest when Demetrius kisses Helena and then she faints, and he runs away; moments later, she gets up and follows him while the fairies leave the gallery. Puck returns to his trapeze and passes the love-in-idleness to Oberon as he swings along the side of him. Titania also makes great use of her bower, which is nothing more than a hammock with its ostrich feathers which can be lowered. This most unusual of bowers is the site of much erotic activity.

The next scene is also one filled with eroticism. Lysander sings "Fair Love" to the accompaniment of a guitarist. While Hermia lets Lysander know that he should lie at a greater distance from her out of a sense of modesty, Lysander comes closer to her and pulls her to the stage floor and kisses her. She at this point decides to make him stop his amorous advances. The music of the guitarist continues until they fall asleep.

After the singing of the assified Bottom awakens Titania, she begins to woo Bottom with great intensity. In order to emphasize the vulgar intensity of this scene, an actor places his arm between Bottom's legs in order to signify his virility. Halio quotes David Selbourne who writes, "The arm is moved in phallic pride" between Bottom's legs while paper plates and streamers come down from the gallery. Bottom makes a neighing sound and raises his arms as one would do after enacting a heroic feat. Oberon and Puck swing on trapeze during this unbridled expression of eroticism to the accompaniment of Mendelssohn's "Wedding March," which functions as a biting bit of satire of 19th-century traditions. Brook obviously wants to challenge theatergoers' conventional understanding of this play through his subversive reading of *A Midsummer Night's Dream*, but the most significant point to remember is the celebratory quality of the actor's actions. One really cannot underestimate the theatrical influence of Brook's production of this play because of its radically transgressive reading of this text.

Significant Theatrical Productions

Perhaps the next really significant theatrical production of *A Midsummer Night's Dream* was Robert Lepage's 1992 version at the Royal National Theatre. Lepage wished to have *A Midsummer Night's Dream* take his audience back to the origins of existence and to form links between the uncivilized world and the civilized one; therefore, Lepage creates a violent sexual union between a sexually ambivalent Puck and a fairy with a blue face at the beginning of the second act in what amounts to group sex in the mud and the loud noise of Bottom and Titania engaging in sexual relations. As Halio points out, with so much physical interaction between characters, both audience members and actors found it difficult to focus on what was said and done by the actors and what was the connection between the two. This issue constituted a significant difference

Sexuality in *A Midsummer Night's Dream*

Olivia de Havilland, Mickey Rooney, Dick Powell, and James Cagney, from the cast of the 1935 film version of A Midsummer Night's Dream, *gather together with Warner Brothers executives.* © Copyright Bettmann/Corbis.

between Lepage's and Brook's production of this play, for when the actors in Brook's production did not perform, they looked over the parapet of the white box and listened carefully to their fellow actors, and finally, while Lepage's production appeared to be quite unconventional by most 20th-century theatrical standards, he did try to maintain the primacy of the play's text.

Adrian Noble directed the last groundbreaking production of *A Midsummer Night's Dream* with the Royal Shakespeare Company. In this production the dominant concept of the play concerned a descent into one's unconscious. The significance of the unconscious seemed to have been represented powerfully in Puck's interactions with Oberon, for no sooner had Oberon and Puck planned how to punish Titania for not relinquishing the Indian boy, Puck kissed Oberon on the lips, which was clearly a homoerotic overture that was not developed in the course of the play. Moreover, the disorientation of the young lovers in the woods corresponded to the forest symbolically as the unconscious. When Jane Edwardes reviewed this play in [the magazine] *Time Out*, she believed that Robert Lepage at the National as Noble grounded his production in the dreams of the characters' supposed sexual desires and covert fears. However, while Lepage's dreamworld had mud and water, Noble and Antony Ward's dreamworld consisted of entrances and appearances and disappearances, which led provocatively into the realm of the characters' unconsciousness. In the final analysis, this production concerned Hippolyta's dream. Whatever one makes of Lepage's dream of *A Midsummer Night's Dream*, one can be sure that it would be a psychoanalyst's delight.

Michael Hoffman's Film

The next really significant film version of *A Midsummer Night's Dream* arrived in 1999 with [director] Michael Hoffman's star-studded cast which included the likes of Michelle Pfeiffer as Titania, Kevin Kline as Bottom, Rupert Everett as Oberon, and Christian Bale as Demetrius among others. This particular version, set in Italy at [the rural village of] Monte Athena in the 1890s, is lushly appointed with all of the accoutrements of a magnificent manor with exquisitely manicured lawns and gushing fountains.

When Egeus appears with Hermia, Lysander, and Demetrius before Theseus, the lawgiver of Monte Athena, in order to have the marriage of Hermia to Demetrius adjudicated, Theseus opens a legal text in order to consult it; despite the juridical importance of this meeting, even here Lysander played by Dominic West and Demetrius played by Christian Bale engage in a shoving match when Demetrius tells Lysander that he should marry Egeus. Given the gravity of the situation, Egeus gives Hermia time to consult her feelings. Stephen

Buhler asserts, "Theseus is portrayed as empathetic and solicitous, expressing deep concern about Hermia's suitability for the veil and deciding to remonstrate privately with Demetrius and Egeus in response to Hermia's clear displeasure."

Soon thereafter the young lovers are in the Athenian woods, and Lysander and Hermia are tired from walking and decide to sleep, but Lysander quickly becomes amorous removing all of his clothes and even sporting an unseen erection, causing Hermia to give him a petticoat with which to cover himself. Buhler believes that Lysander appears defenseless in his makeshift loincloth or his diaper that is too big for him, which was made of one of Hermia's slips. This viewer thought that Lysander is never vulnerable in the least; rather he functions as a gorgeous piece of eye candy for women and gay men who would watch the film. Despite the fact that the play is set within the late Victorian period, once the lovers are in the woods, often thought of as a metaphor for the characters' unconscious or libido, they become less inhibited. As evidenced by the fight in the mud pond between Helena and Hermia, Buhler argues that Hoffman reduces Hermia and Helena's relationship to "merely mud-wrestling over men" by his deleting Helena's lines (III.ii.203–214) in which she recounts their long ... friendship during which they spent time working on their samplers. For a moment eroticism becomes a parody of itself, for the men almost fall into the pond, no longer voyeurs but participants in the muddy melee as Lysander approaches its edge to pull Helena from the mess.

Happily, Oberon is concerned about Helena, and, ironically, it is because of her unhappiness that Oberon instructs Puck to place the love juice on the man who does not love her. Buhler opines that as an openly gay man, Rupert Everett, in both his film roles and in his personal life, can make decisions about heterosexual relationships with an emotional detachment, and while there is no overt homoeroticism in this particular film version, there is a certain homosociality among the rude mechanicals as Bottom's marriage is surely a loveless one, and it is only through his camaraderie with his fellow friends that he has any sense of community. Reinhardt's and Dieterle's 1935 film version originally planned to include a disapproving Mrs. Bottom, but perhaps having James Cagney, star of gangster films from the 1930s, take the role of Bottom obviated that possibility.

The character of Bottom surely satisfies Titania in Hoffman's film version. His erection admirably impresses Titania and her train of fairies. When Titania and Bottom engage in sexual relations, she climbs on top of him.... Buhler implies that Titania is unaccustomed to intense erotic pleasure, perhaps suggesting that the fairy king may be less than adequate in the lovemaking department.

Finally, the issue of gender identity is addressed in the performance of "Pyramus and Thisbe" in which [Francis] Flute plays the role of the young woman. Hoffman stresses the anxiety with which Flute ([played by actor] Sam Rockwell) experiences performing the role of Thisbe. Flute tries to speak in a falsetto voice despite the audience's laughter, and he mangles his lines as he talks about "kissing the wall's stones," a slang term for testicles. It is also interesting to point out that [Tom] Snout looks concerned when Flute has his sword pointed at his groin area, but the rude mechanicals make it through the playlet in spite of themselves.

An All-Male Cast

In the performance of Shakespeare's plays, everything old is new again with the all-male version of *A Midsummer Night's Dream* that [director] Edward Hall, no relation to Peter, produced at the Watermill Theatre and Propeller at the Brooklyn Academy in March 2004. All objects on the stage are either black or white and illuminated by a dingy blue light. The center of the stage is bare except for a wooden box with a mirror on top of it. The costumes of the actors reflect this black-and-white contrast of the set. All of the actors wear white union suits with black shoes; some, however, wear black corsets attached to them over their union suits, and each of the actors has a harmonica that he wears around his neck. Jane Collins asserts that Hall made casting choices that had nothing to do with the actors' physical characteristics which would diminish the differences between their being perceived as either male or female.

While the sex of the actor is of no significance in this version of *A Midsummer Night's Dream*, Collins argues, "The fairy world is marked by campy song and dance numbers that defy the pejorative use of 'fairy' to describe gay men by enacting those cultural stereotypes. These fairies really do act like 'fairies.'" At the same time these actors are quite adept in using body language in order to indicate their femininity. As interest in early modern theatrical practices becomes more popular, more and more of all-male or even all-female versions of early modern dramatic texts will inevitably occur.

Social Issues in Literature

CHAPTER 3

Contemporary Perspectives on Sexuality

Adolescent Sexuality Is a Universal Concern

Monique Long

Monique Long is a law student at the University of the West Indies at Cave Hill, Barbados. She is a member of the Vice Chancellor's Ambassador Corps—a group of students who advocate for HIV/AIDS awareness and promotion of Caribbean integration.

Long investigates global studies of adolescent sexuality, concluding that similarities in views, attitudes, and responses to youthful sex are similar worldwide. One's sexuality, she writes, is a concern regardless of race, religion, culture, or any other category. Adolescents all over the world experiment to learn who they are as sexual beings. Two contrasting adult responses to adolescent sexuality are to counsel abstinence or to advocate for the use of birth control. While specific measures to curb youthful sexuality may be barbaric, such as female genital mutilation, or "civilized," such as purity rings and chastity vows, no known measures completely curtail adolescents in their quest for sexual identity.

The question of one's sexuality transcends religious, racial, and cultural differences. Irrespective of skin colour, gender, gods worshipped, or how different cultures portray it, people everywhere explore their sexuality. Especially during adolescence, in a bid to discover and embrace who they truly are, questions such as "what is sex?" and "who am I as a sexual being?" plague the minds of young women and men as they struggle through the years between childhood and adulthood.

Monique Long, "Adolescent Sexuality," *UN Chronicle*, December 2010, Copyright © 2010 by United National Publications. All rights reserved. Reproduced by permission.

Across the world, adolescent sexuality is an important social and medical topic. Statistics show that most boys and girls become sexually active at around the age of fifteen or earlier. Many interpretations of adolescent sexuality can be examined in the way that different cultures adopt the practices of abstinence and contraception.

Adolescent Sexual Behaviour

In 2002, the World Health Organization (WHO) examined sexual trends among fifteen-year-old students from thirty-five countries. The study showed that while the percentage of boys who engaged in sexual intercourse was often higher than that of girls, there were emerging trends indicating that as many or more girls than boys were sexually active when they turned fifteen. However, while this changing trend was registered, the age at which most boys first had intercourse remained younger than that of girls, showing that gender can influence adolescent sexuality. The study also indicated that the median age of first intercourse in most countries was sixteen to nineteen years for girls, and seventeen to nineteen years for boys. In [the African nation of] Chad girls have their first sexual intercourse at 15.9 years, and boys at 18.8. Sub-Saharan Africa presented similar statistics that contradicted those gathered by WHO in which all countries recorded girls as becoming sexually involved at the same age or at an older age than boys.

How could this be? In parts of Africa, the prevalence of rape and the custom of early marriage regulate sexual activity. In South Africa, for instance, 116 in every one hundred thousand women have reported being raped; and in the rest of Africa, 42 per cent of women between fifteen and twenty-four years of age were married before they turned eighteen, often to men who are up to fifteen years their senior.

In examining adolescent sexuality and sexual behaviour, many cultures differ on the practices of abstinence and contraception.

Abstinence

The practice of abstinence is subject to cultural, social, and religious differences, and its relevance and effectiveness are always in question. However, whatever its cultural variation, abstinence plays a major role in the regulation of adolescent sexual behaviour.

In some developed countries, abstinence is characterized by purity rings and chastity vows aimed at preventing sexual intercourse prior to marriage, while in some developing countries abstinence is enforced through female genital mutilation and other traditional practices, which are detrimental to the sexual development of adolescents.

The 2008 "Youth Reproductive and Sexual Health" report by the United States Agency for International Development noted that the abstinence rate for women in Africa varied between 34 per cent in [the Democratic Republic of the] Congo and 96 per cent in Eritrea, Ethiopia, and Senegal, while in Armenia and Vietnam it was 100 per cent. In Eritrea, before the onset of puberty, 39 per cent of girls had gone through infibulation, a particular method of genital mutilation considered to promote abstinence of intercourse due to painful consequences.

Despite the high rates of abstinence in Africa, the HIV/AIDS epidemic remains rampant, forcing one to consider whether abstinence could be a practical long-term solution against the spread of sexually transmitted diseases. A study in the United States found that adolescents who took abstinence pledges would delay sexual intercourse for less than two years, but upon becoming sexually active they were one-third less likely to use contraception than their non-abstaining counterparts.

Although cultures within both developed and developing countries approach abstinence differently, it appears that neither female genital mutilation nor abstinence vows play a role

Teens and their parents stand by an altar as the teens prepare to receive rings from their parents during a purity ring ceremony in Franklin, Tennessee. The ceremony involves teenage boys and girls who take a pledge to abstain from sex before marriage. © Marvi Lacar/Getty Images.

in preventing the untimely initiation of sexual activity; instead, they seem to delay unhealthy sexual decisions rather than prevent them.

Contraception

Contraceptive use is directly affected by sex education, the availability of contraception, its cost, and cultural practices.

A WHO study found that more than 70 per cent of sexually active adolescents in thirty-five countries used condoms. In most cases, the use of condoms by boys surpassed that of girls. The fact that boys were more likely to use condoms could be indicative of the belief in most cultures that girls were expected to remain chaste, while boys were not, and were thus better informed than their female counterparts.

However, another study uncovered an alternate reality in Africa, Asia, and the Caribbean. In many cases, less than 25 per cent of youth admitted to using modern forms of contraception. Contraceptive use was found to be highest among older women with higher levels of education and living in urbanized areas. Thus, during adolescence, contraceptive use was low and further influenced by social class and education levels.

As adolescents fight internal battles when they come to embrace their sexual identities, they are also forced to grapple with the influence of peers, family, cultural beliefs, and the media. Despite the differences in their experiences and the obstacles they face, all adolescents eventually come to an understanding of who they are as sexual beings. Adolescent sexuality is, and will continue to be, a topic of debate and interest. Regardless of a particular country or culture, similarities in the views, intentions, and practices regarding adolescent sexuality can be found around the world. Clearly, adolescent sexuality is a universal issue.

More Grey than Gay

Apoorva Dutt

Apoorva Dutt is the Sunday features writer at DNA (Daily News & Analysis) newspaper in Mumbai, India.

Dutt states that while everyone is interested in other people's sex lives, the manner in which people classify others as straight, gay, or otherwise is losing its meaning. Many modern men and women defy such classifications and live lives on their own terms. Dutt cites three Indian men and women who reject sexual labels and stereotypes. Karan Mahendru has been with people of both sexes before settling down with his present girlfriend. He boldly states that his sexuality does not define him. Aishwarya, a young gay woman, rejects the lesbian, gay, bisexual, and transgender (LGBT) community, insisting that her sexuality is only one part of who she is and that it does not define her. Neeraj is a happily married man who is attracted to other men. He and his wife are "best friends" and see nothing odd about being married, despite Neeraj's predilections. Marriage they say, is not always stereotypical, and a perfect marriage is merely a fantasy created by Hollywood, Dutt reports.

What, and who, you do in bed is of immense interest to everyone. We're on the lookout for telltale signs—a too-colourful wardrobe, a macho interest in action flicks, or a too-short haircut on a girl—to figure out where we can place someone on the sexuality spectrum.

But many people—some would say most—live on the edges of the broad classifications of straight and gay, bisexual

---

Apoorva Dutt, "More grey than gay; Some reject the LGBT community, some reject sexuality as a necessity for a happy marriage, and others reject the need to define their sexuality at all. Apoorva Dutt talks to three individuals who march to their own beat," *DNA (Daily News & Analysis)*, March 6, 2011. Copyright © 2011 by DNA (Daily News & Analysis). All rights reserved. Reproduced by permission.

and lesbian. Living on your own terms can sometimes mean even rejecting the 'alternate' definitions a liberal society places before you.

Spare Me the Labels, Please

Karan Mahendru is a 54-year-old with a colourful past. The thespian—who now lives in a sprawling two-bedroom apartment with his girlfriend Sakshi—has travelled to four continents, been a part of a travelling theatre group that performed in front of the pope, was married twice, and trained to be an acrobat with the Cirque du Soleil. His sexual past is as varied: "I've slept with tall men, thin women, short trannies, you name it," he guffaws. "I've been alive a long time, what do you expect!"

Mahendru often lapses into an academic tone while talking about his sexual history, as though recounting a lifelong anthropological study. "I started very conventionally; I had a girlfriend through college for four years. She was a sweet girl. I fancied myself to be in love with her, we made marriage plans and all that. After that I left India. I was studying in the U.S. for five years after that. We, of course, broke up. I had a brief flirtation with being 'gay', going to rallies and parties, campaigning for rights, having gay-only dinner parties. It was great fun. A friend introduced me to cross-dressing."

Mahendru surveys a rack of dresses in his bedroom cupboard fondly. The dresses, mostly wrapped in plastic, are gauzy and bright. "I just keep them for old times' sake; cross-dressing is less fun now. Plus Sakshi's not really into it."

After his first marriage floundered because of financial disagreements, Mahendru went online. "Shaadi.com, the saviour of all Indian bachelors," he quips. When even his second marriage went belly-up, Mahendru cast the whole institution aside. "The way I see it, when we stop loving each other, no piece of paper can get the love back."

So where on the sexuality spectrum would Mahendru put himself if he had to? "Nowhere! Society loves classifying every individual, so that it doesn't have to trouble itself with actually understanding each one. Who's gay, who's bisexual, who's straight, and who's a deviant. Even within the LGBT community—who's on top, who's the man or the woman in the relationship, who's the dyke. Spare me these classifications. We're all sexual beings."

My Sexuality Doesn't Define Me

Twenty-two-year-old Aishwarya lives in Mumbai and works in films. She was thirteen when she realised she was gay. "I had a crush on a girl, so I just put two and two together," she says dryly. Aishwarya's story lacks the tears and drama of usual coming-out narratives. "I was gay, I told my parents. They had already kind of figured it out—parents always know, whether you're smoking, drinking, or attracted to girls. So they supported me. They've never judged me."

Aishwarya points out that a common hurdle for the gay community in India is that "they take so long to come to terms with their sexual identity that it takes years for them to get around to dating". Aishwarya dated women—and men—over the next nine years, and admits that she's actually had more relationships with men than women. "Everybody dabbles. I dabbled as well. It was always better with women though, more natural and comfortable, and they f---ed with my mind better, so I figured I must be gay."

Aishwarya allows that the gay movement has a long way to go—"We're still judged. For example, I hate how straight people think that just because I'm gay, I'll hit on anyone and everyone. I'm not indiscriminate."

But she has a fundamental problem with the 'LGBT community'. "I don't put myself out there with this 'community'. I've been to gay parties, and meetings—something my girlfriend at the time insisted on—but once you differentiate yourself as a community, and once you define yourself purely on your sexual orientation, how can you ask to be treated the same as everyone else? This 'I'm different' motto is detrimental." She insists that her sexuality is incidental to who she is as an individual. "Gay is one of the many things I am."

Gay Physically, Not Emotionally

'Gay marriage' can take a whole new meaning in an Indian context. Stories are darkly told of those pushed into a marriage because of their 'perverted' tastes—stories which end in tearful recriminations. But these stories are as unique as the people who live them—like Jenine and Neeraj.

They were both 25 when they got married in 1992 in Chennai. The Tamilian bride was a PhD holder who had just finished her first year in a medical research institute, and Neeraj was freshly returned from a stint in Chicago studying theatre. "I had my first relationship with a man there," he stops, uncomfortable. Jenine puts her hand on top of his. "Neeraj was in love before we met, with someone else."

Jenine, like any other happily married woman, vividly remembers her wedding day. "My three best friends were chattering and teasing me about *suhag raat* and all that nonsense. I was nervous because I hadn't known him for very long", she gestures at Neeraj, who is reclining on the sofa next to her, "and I didn't know what would happen."

Jenine married not knowing that her future husband was sexually attracted to men. Neeraj continued to meet men—some friends, some strangers—on the side after his marriage. It was a year after their wedding that Jenine realised what was going on.

"I was in shock," she says, recalling the time when she found out Neeraj was cheating on her with men. "We had a child by then, I felt betrayed on our child's behalf as well. I left immediately. But of course, as you know, I came back." Neeraj and Jenine had developed a friendship that sustained the couple through the year and a half that they were apart. They wrote to each other constantly, talked every day, and Jenine returned, a decision she calls "the best of my life". "He was, and is, my best friend. I couldn't have asked for a better companion and father."

Neeraj still sees men, but at any mention of the word gay, he shakes his head vigorously. "I am not gay! I am not gay at all. I might have been, once, when I was in Chicago, maybe then you could have called me that ... but now, I would not choose any man over my wife. I love her and my child; this is the family I am committed to." He goes on to say that though "sexually" he is attracted to men, "emotionally and spiritually" he considers himself straight—"My love for my wife is proof of this," he concludes.

How does his wife deal with his sexual orientation? "We don't have sex! That's fairly normal for a couple married for so long, no?" she laughs. "I don't judge him for who he is. It's a need that I realised I could never fulfill. Marriage is not black and white, to expect everything from your spouse is a Hollywood dream."

What Do Men Really Want?

Eric Jaffe

Eric Jaffe is a writer living in the New York metropolitan area.

In the following viewpoint, Jaffe investigates the question of what men want. Although men have always been stereotyped as only being interested in sex, Jaffe cites numerous studies showing that men are much more complicated. When it comes to the female body, for example, preferred body type can vary widely worldwide. Jaffe maintains that another stereotype holds that women usually say "I love you" first in a relationship, but studies find that the reverse is true. When it comes to long-term relationships, Jaffe reports, studies found that nonsexual intimacy, such as cuddling and kissing, can be as important to male satisfaction as regular sex. Such results suggest to Jaffe that men want the same things that women do—love and sex—and that men rarely fit society's stereotypical mold.

The study of male sexuality really should have ended in 1989. That year psychologists Russell Clark and Elaine Hatfield reported the results of a social experiment conducted on the campus of Florida State University. For the study they recruited young women to approach male students at random and have a brief conversation. Average-looking women, mind you—"moderately attractive," even "slightly unattractive"—in casual clothes. No supermodels; no stilettos; no bare midriffs. It was important that the young man remain coherent. The ladies all told their guy they'd seen him around campus. They

---

Eric Jaffe, "What do men really want? There's the stereotype. And there's the reality. But the reality about what men want in women and from women is getting more complex by the minute. Men and their motives—stop the presses!—are evolving," *Psychology Today*, March–April 2012. Copyright © 2012 by Psychology Today. All rights reserved. Reproduced by permission.

said they found him very attractive. Then some asked their man on a date. Some asked him to come over that night. And some asked him, point blank, to go to bed.

Cue the incoherence. Nearly 70 percent of men agreed to visit the lady's apartment, and 75 percent accepted the sexual proposition. At least one man asked why wait until the night. Another checked his mental calendar and said he couldn't today but what about tomorrow. Another who refused on account of being married apologized for having to refuse on account of being married. Meanwhile just half the men agreed to go out sometime. Extrapolating the finding to the real world means that on any given first date, the man would sooner sleep with the hostess than dine with his companion.

The study seemed to confirm every stereotype anyone ever held about what men want (for the purposes of this article, what heterosexual men want). We want women. Now, please—although tonight will do. At worst tomorrow. We want them like that old Army poster with the finger pointing outward. We want you. We want you like we're all Uncle Sam, and dammit if the Germans aren't at it again. Pack up the lab equipment, please, shut off the lights, and move on to more important behavioral studies. Like finding out who drinks "lots of pulp" Tropicana.

But the research did not stop there. What psychologists discovered is that underneath the simplicity, we men can be surprisingly complicated. We want women, yes, and we want sex. But we don't always want a slender frame and sharp curves. Sometimes we want a good personality. And a good romantic comedy. And to cuddle. This is laboratory science talking—not Hallmark or four martinis.

And our motives for sex have diversified (as have women's)—a reality Hatfield now calls "one of our planet's most important new developments." We want sex, but sometimes we want it to enhance the emotional relationship. We want to say "I love you" before you do, some of us; we want to race you to love, and win. We want to love you so much that when we see a pretty face we think it's less pretty than we would if we didn't love you.

It doesn't take a psychologist to know what men want. But give a whole lot of them a whole lot of time and you begin to understand the considerable nuance that governs what men want. Some people like pulp in their orange juice, after all.

The Body

Often while walking the streets of Manhattan I adjust both the pace and position of my stride so as to follow close behind, but not illegally close behind, an attractive woman. I must stress here to my girlfriend and mother that I do not do this to admire the view. All right, so partly I do this to admire the view. But another part of me likes to observe the reactions we—we're a caravan, now—receive from the menfolk we pass. To walk this way is to witness the spasmodic necks and detoured eyes and high-pitched whistled salutes and deep, perfumed inhalations and even, at times, affected indifference that together form the grand choreography of male desire. The performance is a haphazard one, and far creepier to the audience than to the actors, but it remains sincere as instinct.

When evolutionary psychologists review this show, they find evidence for a universal male urge to reproduce. A woman's figure is a hallmark of her fertility, they argue, and men subconsciously know it. Researchers have documented a widespread, magnetic male attraction to a waist-to-hip ratio of .7—the classic hourglass. An eye-tracking study last year found that men start to evaluate a woman's hourglassness within the first 200 milliseconds of viewing, which, based on my pedestrian observations, seems slow.

But to call this desire universal is to ignore a great deal of competing information. While men in developed societies go numb for sinuous curves, those in many developing countries surrender to a larger, more parallel contour. Plumpness may be a sign of poor health in the West, but elsewhere it's a sign that a woman has access to money and food. Some cultures even prefer a body type that health experts consider clinically overweight. And when a man changes culture, he adjusts his preferred measurements accordingly.

"I think one of the biggest myths that has been perpetuated by some evolutionary psychologists—though not all—is that there is one 'man,' or 'men,' with universal behaviors," says psychologist Viren Swami of the University of Westminster in London. "In most socioeconomically developed societies, there is—not surprisingly—a preference for relatively slender women. In many developing societies, on the other hand, the ideal female body size is heavier." That may be little solace to some Western women, but as Swami has found, even Western males demonstrate malleability in figure preference.

A few years ago, Swami and an international group of psychologists led by Martin Tovee of Newcastle University surveyed the female body preferences of men (and women) in the United Kingdom and among the Zulu of South Africa. Participants flipped through a photo booklet of real but blurry-faced women wearing tight gray leotards and rated each one. The Britons gave high marks to slender curves, while the Zulu enjoyed heavier bodies. Then Zulu migrants living in Britain had their turn with the booklets—and chose bodies right in between.

As their social networks changed, so did male preferences. Maybe men don't lock their eyes onto 36-24-36 like some broken slot machine after all, but instead possess a "flexible behavioral repertoire" that adapts sexual preferences to changing environments, the researchers conclude in *Evolution and Human Behavior*. A subsequent study corroborated the shortcomings of a global thin ideal, as well as the role of Western media in propagating it.

Women need not move to Mpolweni to find such flexibility in action. Even among developed societies, shape preferences vary sharply. In countries like Britain or Denmark, where women have achieved social and economic independence, a low waist-to-hip ratio is less important to men than it is in places where women rely more heavily on men for resource acquisition, such as Greece or Portugal, Swami and other researchers find. The more resources a woman can gather on her own, the less men care whether or not her figure conforms to the supposed ideal.

Time and chance can change a man's physical ideals as much as place. One research team recently compared the measurements of *Playboy* Playmates of the Year from 1960 to 2000 to economic conditions in the United States over the same period and found that tougher times called for larger playmates. A 2005 study in *Psychological Science* reported that men who were manipulated to feel either hungry or poor preferred heavier female figures—a sign that, according to the researchers, resource availability can "influence preferences for potential mates" even among Western males in a wealthy culture. In other words, we can live in New York but possess a Zulu state of mind.

The Attraction

Just as our bodily ideals aren't stuck on the hourglass, neither is our general desire stuck on the body. A survey conducted around the time of the Clark-Hatfield study reported that about a third of men have imagined sexual encounters with more than 1,000 different women. In our minds, at our best, we are not Einstein but Warren Beatty. Swami's studies support the concept of dynamic attractiveness—the idea that no matter our age or body preference, looks are but a single line of code in a complex algorithm of attraction, alongside others defining sense of humor, core beliefs, personality, and more.

"There is an urgent need to expand what we mean by 'attractiveness' to include a much broader array of factors than physical traits alone," says Swami. Studies indicate that a majority of people are concerned with their appearance, "but studies also indicate that attraction and relationship formation are often more strongly predicted by factors other than physical appearance. Physical attractiveness might matter in the absence of social interaction, but once social interaction takes place, the importance of appearance diminishes rapidly."

Swami and colleagues recently showed a couple thousand young men in London pictures of young women accompanied by brief personality vignettes. The guys rated each image and also indicated the largest and smallest female figures they found appealing, effectively producing a range of acceptable attractiveness. Men who looked at the images while reading positive personality briefs expanded their ranges, while men who read negative bios shrunk theirs, the team reports in the *Journal of Social Psychology*. The greatest range change occurred with heavier women, judged much more physically attractive when paired with an appealing character trait like openness or emotional stability.

Of course, it's easy for men to say on paper that they care about personality. What really matters is how things unfold when they're two feet from a push-up bra and nice-smelling, fruit-conditioned hair.

Northwestern University psychologists Paul Eastwick and Eli Finkel recently arranged a speed-dating event for 163 university guys and gals and had them indicate beforehand what they wanted in a mate: attractiveness, earning potential, or personality qualities. The men—no surprise—overwhelmingly said they wanted looks. But when they got to the table something changed. Eastwick and Finkel discovered that pre-event ideals failed to predict a person's true romantic interests.

In other words, saying you value physical attractiveness doesn't make you more likely to feel a spark with those you consider physically attractive, the researchers report in the *Journal of Personality and Social Psychology*. "When men say they care about physical attractiveness more than women, what that should mean is that attractiveness buys you more romantic desirability if you're a woman than if you're a man," says Eastwick, now at Texas A&M University. "Our study showed that in fact that wasn't the case."

A subsequent study led by Eastwick confirmed that men don't always recognize what they want in a woman. The researchers asked male participants to list a few traits they like in a lady. Then some of them had a brief, live interaction with a female who matched these interests, while others had a similar interaction with someone who didn't.

As the team concludes in a recent issue of the *Journal of Personality and Social Psychology*, male hearts don't seem to care what type of preconceived romantic preferences reside in male heads. (Interestingly, the same effect occurs in female participants.) "There's something about getting that live impression of another person that seems to get in the way of people's use of their ideals," says Eastwick. That something may be the malleability of attraction: A girl with the pretty picture can be too cookie-cutter in person, while one with an average photo can be endearingly cute. "Attractiveness just seems like attractiveness in the abstract," he says.

So we males articulate our desires with the precision of a leaf blower. That may not help our Match.com profiles, but it does support the legend of male complexity. Sociologist Rebecca Plante of Ithaca College says it's a massive oversimplification to think that a man's sexual desire is "as plain as the erection in his pants." Plante has been leading part of a national, multicampus, quantitative, and qualitative study of some 14,000 college students, organized by sociologist Paula England at Stanford, on the culture of hooking up. What Plante has found so far defies all simple expectations: While some guys do view sex and desire as one and the same, many others—even those in the early stages of a casual engagement—want someone they know and trust on a deeper level.

When it comes to long-term relationships, studies have found that nonsexual intimacy can be as important to male satisfaction as regular sex. Such results suggest that men want the same things that women do—love, sex, and intimacy. © B. Sporrer/J. Skowronek/ StockFood Creative/Getty Images.

"We haven't done a good job giving men an emotional language, culturally speaking, to say 'hooking up doesn't work,'" says Plante. "To say, 'I actually like to know my partner. I like to be in a relationship with her. I like to be connected to her. That's what turns me on, more so than that she's attractive.'"

The Commitment

Male stereotypes fail to take into account the importance of what might be called a commitment continuum. At one end are married men, at the other are gigolos, with all shades of monogamous and polygamous moderation in between. The oversight helps perpetuate misunderstandings of what men want.

Yes, physical attractiveness is very important to men, but it's much more important to men prowling for a fling—who, studies show, tend to be younger men—than those after a steady mate. Yes, many men want younger women, but most of those reside on the short-term hall of the spectrum; long-term guys tend to prefer women around their own age. Yes, men like the hourglass figure, but while they focus on the body over the face when looking for sex, the reverse is true for men looking for a relationship, studies report. (Women focus on the face either way.)

Take one recent finding that runs entirely counter to popular wisdom. As the undisputed emotional champion of any relationship, women are supposed to profess their love first. But a group of researchers led by psychologist Joshua Ackerman of MIT found the axiom to be dead wrong. Their surveys of twenty- and thirtysomethings revealed that men say "I love you" first 60 to 70 percent of the time. They even thought about saying it a full six weeks before their mate did. It took about as much time for women to catch up to their men emotionally, in other words, as it took Hemingway to complete *The Sun Also Rises*.

The meaning of the finding, Ackerman and colleagues report in the *Journal of Personality and Social Psychology*, turns on the commitment continuum. In subsequent tests, the researchers discovered that short-term guys felt a decrease in happiness when women declared "I love you" after sex. They'd said it first to score quickly, the finding suggests, and then, having scored, began to realize what they'd done.

But men of the long-term persuasion were as happy to hear the words after sex as women were; when they said "I love you," they meant what women meant. Mark Twain once said the difference between the right and wrong word is the difference between lightning and lightning bug; the difference between the right and wrong commitment context appears to be the difference between love and lover.

"It was interesting to see that it wasn't all men who were conflating love with sex—it was just the short-term-oriented men," says Ackerman. "There are different kinds of men and they mean different kinds of things when they're communicating love."

The longer a man stays long term, the more in touch with his emotional side he may get. The Kinsey Institute recently conducted an international survey of more than 1,000 middle-aged couples who had, on average, been together 25 years. The researchers measured each partner's relationship and sexual satisfaction on a number of variables. Some of the findings were obvious—sexual functioning, for instance, was strongly related to male sexual satisfaction—but others were highly unexpected.

One "striking" finding, to borrow the report's own word, was a very strong connection between a man's relationship satisfaction and his frequency of physical intimacy. Not physical intimacy as in sex, but physical intimacy as in kissing, cuddling, and general, not necessarily sexual, caressing. The odds of a man being happy in his relationship increased by a factor of three if he snuggled up regularly.

The researchers were floored and expect the finding to prompt full "reconsideration of the role of physical affection and its meaning for each gender in longer-term relationships." Says Julia Heiman, director of the Kinsey Institute and the study leader, "People really are so willing to accept stereotypes of male promiscuity and inability to commit. That is the problem with stereotyping: It tends not to be 'men in their early 20s'; it tends to be 'all men.' It's just that men are more complicated than that."

Something about being in a relationship even seems to change instinctual male desires. A good deal of evidence suggests that men sense when a woman is primed for reproduction; they can tell she's ovulating, for instance, just by sniffing a T-shirt she wore, and they rate her as more attractive—and, in one classic study of strippers, give her better tips—at these times of the month than at others.

But heightened sensitivity to a woman's sex drive can be dulled by the mere existence of commitment. Florida State psychologists Saul Miller and Jon Maner report in the *Journal of Experimental Social Psychology* that while single men rate a woman as particularly attractive at her peak fertility, men in a long-term relationship consider her less appealing.

"There's an interesting and complex relationship between how committed a man is and how actively he'll try to avoid tempting sexual alternatives," says Maner. "As one example: Men sometimes automatically avert their gaze from tempting alternatives, and they do so without even having to think about it." Maybe that indifference some men show in the presence of attractive women on New York City sidewalks isn't affected at all. Maybe it's affection remembered.

The Complexity

If we are complex—still admittedly if—we don't like to show it. Sometimes our emotional side is so hidden researchers can't find it. A notable mid-'90s study by evolutionary psychologists found that when you ask people what type of infidelity will upset them, men say a sexual tryst more than women, and women an emotional affair more than men. That's Mars and Venus in galactic alignment.

Only problem is, we're on Earth. What the research revealed to those on this planet is that within the male gender the question is far from settled. Envisioning a mate having acrobatic sex with a stranger made only about a quarter of Dutch and German men more upset than picturing her in love with the fellow, and about half of Americans responded the same way.

A recent study of romantic comedies unearthed another emotional surprise. Sure, men reported enjoying sappy movies less than women do—the term *chick flicks* is not on trial here—but that's very different from concluding that men don't like them at all. Psychologist Richard Jackson Harris of

Kansas State University found that actual men liked seeing a romantic comedy on a date much more than women thought "most men" would.

And when men were asked to choose which of the film's scenes they'd like to enact, 40 percent chose a romantic encounter (read: kissing or caressing without intercourse) while another 15 percent chose an intimate conversation. Only 20 percent chose a full-on sex scene. We may have 1,000 or so sexual fantasies, but only in some of them are we the cable guy who arrives just as you're getting out of the shower. In others we're Paul Rudd.

To some degree, notions of male simplicity persist, despite growing evidence to the contrary, due to the very nature of masculinity. A recent series of experiments described in *Current Directions in Psychological Science* conclude that manhood is both elusive and tenuous. In one experiment, test participants associated the loss of manhood with social, impermanent things, like letting someone down, as opposed to physical things, like growing weak with age. So manhood must be earned by demonstration, and it must be demonstrated repeatedly, until we've shielded our vulnerability behind a haze of one-dimensional sexuality.

"Men seemed to have a heightened sense of the precariousness of the male gender role," says University of South Florida psychologist Jennifer Bosson, the paper's lead author. "We haven't found many men willing to admit that my manhood is often in question, but when you ask men in general if manhood is something that's easy to lose and hard to attain, they agree that's the case." Or, as the Kinsey Institute's Julia Heiman puts it: "Heterosexual men have a little trouble saying they really like kissing and cuddling."

When the roles were reversed in the 1989 Clark-Hatfield study and men were doing the sexual offering, about half the women accepted the date. Very, very few agreed to come over that night. Not a single one agreed to go to bed. "You've got to be kidding," was a common reply. "What is wrong with you?" was another. Some things haven't changed much in the recent past, and aren't likely to: In replications of the experiment, albeit on paper, researchers have consistently found that men are far more likely than women to accept the casual sexual offer.

But some things have changed. One re-creation of the classic study, which was conducted by an international group of researchers and published in *Human Nature*, found that men are much more likely to date a woman than they had been in 1989. Although the updated study was conducted on paper, not in person, it included a larger and more diverse population of men, and it varied the attractiveness of the sex solicitor. More men were willing to date a "slightly unattractive" woman than were willing to sleep with an "exceptionally attractive" woman, 87 percent to about 82.

The researchers also found that women were willing to hop into bed too—a full 24 percent—if the man was good-looking enough. Another re-creation of the original experiment, conducted by Michigan psychologist Terri Conley, discovered similar behavioral shifts. She reports in the *Journal of Personality and Social Psychology* that two in five women accept a proposition if they think the man will be good enough in bed.

"Social commentators tend to be extremists. They view the world as, one, men and women are identical, or two, we are different species. There is little sense of nuance," says Elaine Hatfield now, looking back on why her findings produced such a strong response. "I think both men and women want love and sex. Some men pretend to be macho. But under the right conditions both men and women admit to being more complex than the stereotypes would have it."

Americans Are Still Not Honest About Sexuality

Bob Minor

Bob Minor is a columnist for Liberty Press. *He is Professor Emeritus of Religious Studies at the University of Kansas, Lawrence. He is the author of eight books, including* When Religion Is an Addiction; Gay and Healthy in a Sick Society; *and* Scared Straight: Why It's So Hard to Accept Gay People and Why It's So Hard to Be Human.

Minor surveys the state of sexual attitudes in America in 2012 and is disappointed in his findings. Most people are afraid to talk about sexual freedoms, he finds, and thus they allow politicians and other authority figures to bully them into acceding to out-of-touch ideas. Sex is still a convoluted topic in America, and few people will discuss it honestly in public, Minor maintains. Therefore, numerous misconceptions and outdated ideas prevail. Minor lists the numerous ways in which sex is distorted by politicians, media, advertisers, preachers, and ordinary citizens. He believes that Americans still have a long way to go in order to adopt healthy and realistic attitudes toward sexual activity.

There's no better time than Valentine's Day to assess the state of sex in the U.S. You know, the sexual activity that raises fear among leaders of the religious right-wing that it might actually be popular even among their own.

A Convoluted Topic

Republican right-wing presidential candidate Rick Santorum is the latest political exploiter of this terror of sexuality, pontificating in a January [2012] interview that states should re-

Bob Minor, "Minor Details: Sex in 2012," *Liberty Press*, February 2012. Copyright © 2012 by Robert Minor. All rights reserved. Reproduced by permission.

gain the right to outlaw birth control. Contraceptives are, he preaches, "a license to do things in a sexual realm that is counter to how things are supposed to be."

This is out of touch with the reported ideas and practices of the vast majority of Americans. Even among members of the historically most rabid anti-contraception institution, the Roman Catholic Church, women favoring the expansion of birth control poll around 90%.

Yet the rhetoric of erotophobia [fear of eroticism] seems effective. It even upsets enough people who don't agree with Santorum's crowd, scaring most into not speaking up to defend their actual private practices. We appear to have made little public progress in spite of what really goes on in our bedrooms.

In 2008, historian Dagmar Herzog in *Sex in Crisis: The New Sexual Revolution and the Future of American Politics* puzzled over why "it has been so hard for Americans loudly to defend sexual rights even if they definitely enjoy having them. This," she observed, "creates an echo chamber in which the bullies get to set the terms of the debate."

In the U.S. in 2012 sex is still one of the most convoluted topics, and that is because participating in sexual activity doesn't mean one has developed a healthy sense of what their personal sexuality and its related activities mean to them. The messages that come at all of us from our culture and its authorities are still so mixed, confused, and consumer driven, that what we're told is actual sexual activity is buried under widespread distress, guilt, disappointment and fear.

As long as that's true, attitudes toward sexual activity and our ability to stand up clearly for our sexual practices will be closeted, muted, or embarrassing. Sadly, in spite of the so-called sexual revolution, the freedom of younger generations, and the conservative counterrevolution, as a country we still find it difficult to think effectively about sex.

"Science" has tried to take over the discussion. Instead of morality, the questions posed are about normalcy, adequacy, and health. People want experts to assure them that their sexual fantasies, activities and frequencies are normal, their "failures" at sexuality are curable, their erections are adequate or need blue pills, their bodily parts are the right shape or size, and more.

Continued Problems with Sex

We still know sex sells, and we practice that salesmanship. We still have media images of what sex should be with actors on the big and small screens who seldom duplicate them at home.

We still believe that sex is a means of getting close to someone, maybe THE means. Yet our actual sexual activities are often distancing or part of desperation to feel close to someone.

We still see people having sex with someone not just because they want to participate in sexual activity or they want to express the closeness they have with that person through sexual activity, but to prove to themselves that they're still attractive and loveable. There's nothing new in the use of sexual activity to cloak a negative self-image.

We still have those who use it as slaves to the consumer-culture's glorification of youth as beauty, to prove that their aging has not diminished their appeal. Youth, after all, sells. Products will restore it. Wrinkles don't; they just happen if you hang around long enough.

We still have a disconnect between what we say is a relationship between sex and love while we hear jokes about and justifications for marriage causing a diminishment of sexual activity between partners.

We still see sexual activity used to express power over another or to participate in the power that another has. Both rape and the attractiveness of the powerful, we know, aren't about sex.

Contemporary Perspectives on Sexuality

We still hear pitiful attempts to relieve guilt over being sexual. Sometimes it appears in outward moralisms; sometimes it's turned inward.

We still have examples of hypocrisy around sexuality among sex's most vehement critics. It takes little psychology to suspect that those who brandish the loudest antisex positions are speaking out of their inability to reconcile with their own practices.

We are still inundated with public efforts to control women's sexuality. Denying women contraception has historically been the best way to do so, guaranteeing that every sexual encounter could result in pregnancy and, through much of history, the chance of death in childbirth.

We still tell men that sex is THE means for a man to get, express, and experience closeness. If a man prefers substituting any of the hundreds of other means of expressing closeness with someone, we still wonder what's wrong with him.

We still use words and phrases that have so many other meanings—intimacy, morality, sleeping with, close to, doing it, getting any, going all the way, scoring, doing the dirty, and cheating on, for example—and know they mean sex.

Still a Long Way to Go

So, in 2012, we're still having sex, but we haven't been able to have conversations about it to discuss what sex is, what it's for, why we're having it, what about it scares us, and how for so many it doesn't seem to do what it's supposed to do. Instead we respond with obsession, guilt, self-blaming, and bad public policy.

We're still hearing moralists and preachers condemning sexual activity as they have for millennia. Their rantings still haven't changed a thing, improved human relationships, or promoted a fully human, fully present, fully sexual understanding of sex and sexuality in the world.

And we still have to struggle to get comprehensive sexual education in our schools. Instead we still have politicians scared to face the fact that statistically "abstinence-only" approaches fail.

Conclusion: In 2012, we still have a long way to go and a lot of courageous thinking to do.

National Sex Education Standards Spark Controversy

Nirvi Shah

Nirvi Shah is a reporter for Education Week *who covers special education, school nutrition, health, safety, and bullying.*

Shah provides an overview of the National Sexuality Education Standards introduced by a number of student health and sexual education groups in 2012. These standards encompass everything from sexting to bullying, but they have provoked controversy from the start. Shah contends that some argue that one set of standards for the entire country is inappropriate, as students in some areas need education in sexuality earlier than others. Further, Shah reports that others debate the value of "abstinence-only" policies that were employed in the 2000s, with some claiming that the abstinence-only policy is effective, while others prefer advocating abstinence in addition to teaching students about safe sex, or what some call "abstinence plus." According to Shah, proponents of national sex education standards argue that sex education in the United States has largely been a mixed bag up until now, and that universal standards will help to solve this issue.

National standards about sexuality, sexual health, and relationships debuted last week (in January 2012) and outline topics students should learn, starting in kindergarten, and that they can build on as they grow older.

The standards—an initiative by groups concerned with student health and sex education—are intended to mimic content standards for other subjects, which introduce concepts

Nirvi Shah, "National Sexuality Standards Would Introduce Subject Early," *Education Week*, January 2012. Copyright © 2012 by Education Week. All rights reserved. Reproduced by permission.

early in school, based on children's ability to understand them, and then add to them grade by grade until graduation.

A Topic Like Every Other

"In every other topic under the sun, you build young people's skills—whether it's math or science," said Debra Hauser, the president of Advocates for Youth, one of the groups involved. "You don't have to call it 'sex ed' in elementary school."

The groups releasing "National Sexuality Education Standards: Core Content and Skills, K–12" are the American Association for Health Education, the American School Health Association, the National Education Association Health Information Network, and the Society of State Leaders of Health and Physical Education.

Coordinating with them in the project was the Future of Sex Education, a partnership of the Washington-based Advocates for Youth; Answer, in Piscataway, N.J.; and the Sexuality Information and Education Council of the United States, or SIECUS, in New York and Washington. The project was funded by the Ford Foundation, in New York; the George Gund Foundation, based in Cleveland; and the Grove Foundation in Los Altos, Calif.

The authors say the standards are the minimum students should know about sexual and relationship health. By the end of 5th grade, for example, students should be able to explain what bodily changes occur during puberty and adolescence; by 8th grade, they should know what rape, incest, and sexual harassment and abuse are; and by the end of 12th grade, they should be able to define emergency contraception, among dozens of other specifics.

The standards also address contemporary issues of social media, sexting [the sending of sexually explicit messages or images by cell phone], and bullying.

Critics say some of the topics are simply too much, too young.

"I think they're having a different definition of age-appropriate than what we would have," said Valerie Huber, the executive director of the National Abstinence Education Association, in Washington. "If a youngster is able to understand something cognitively, does that make it age-appropriate?"

"Abstinence-Only" Debate

The idea for such national standards originated in 2007 with Advocates for Youth, Answer, and SIECUS, which hoped federal spending on abstinence-only sex education would be scrapped, and in its place, standards would be needed to guide educators on how to teach sexuality comprehensively.

The Future of Sex Education partners cite research showing that abstinence-based sex education is ineffective in preventing young people from having sex. A 2007 congressionally mandated study found no statistically significant beneficial effect on the sexual behavior of young people participating in abstinence-based programs.

The groups point out that as many as 25 states have rejected federal money, despite the economic downturn, when it requires an abstinence-only approach to teaching about sexuality.

Abstinence-only lessons are still supported by the federal government, however. While federal money for abstinence-only sex education was allowed to expire earlier in President Barack Obama's tenure, some of that funding was revived via the [Patient Protection and] Affordable Care Act, the 2010 health care overhaul.

In addition, the recently enacted federal spending bill for fiscal 2012 includes a small amount of money for another program that promotes an abstinence-until-marriage approach to sex education.

Gathering Support

While there are no national sex education requirements for K–12 public schools, at least five states already have inquired

A billboard in downtown Baltimore, Maryland, displays a message of abstinence toward teen sex. Researchers are divided about what works best in combating teen pregnancy and what should be part of a nationwide sex education curriculum. © AP Photo/Gail Burton.

about the new standards, which were reviewed and generally backed by officials from an array of agencies and organizations, including the Atlanta-based Centers for Disease Control [and Prevention], the Washington-based Council of Chief State School Officers, and the National Association of State Boards of Education, in Arlington, Va., as well as individuals from several school districts.

"The more kinds of things that are out there like that, it takes away from some of the stigma and 'specialness' about these subjects that shouldn't be there," said Elizabeth Gallun, the supervisor of health education for the Prince George's County, Md., school district. She was one of the reviewers of the standards.

The Future of Sex Education initiative will next tackle a teacher-training program to help better prepare teachers and other personnel who provide sex education.

While her 125,000-student district, just outside Washington, already uses a comprehensive approach to sex education, she said national standards, such as the common core recently developed for mathematics and English/language arts, are invaluable for policy makers everywhere.

Despite the consensus, the new standards appear to reflect among health education and school groups that the debate on what to teach students about sex, and when, is far from settled.

Last year [in 2011], Mississippi—with some of the highest teenage-pregnancy rates in the country—for the first time required districts to teach sex education. Districts must choose from abstinence-only or "abstinence plus" programs, the latter of which includes information about contraceptives and sexually transmitted diseases.

In Texas, districts have been shifting from an abstinence-only approach to abstinence-plus. While just 4 percent of Texas districts had a comprehensive approach to sex education in 2007, that share grew to about 25 percent in 2010, according to a December report in the *Houston Chronicle*.

The National Sexuality Education Standards takes the opposite approach from that of some sex education classes, which try to scare students away from sex by talking about disease or death, Ms. Hauser of Advocates for Youth said.

"Sexuality is part of who we are as human beings. If you demonize it when you're young, it becomes much harder when you get older," she said.

In addition, the new curricular guidelines seek to reshape ideas about sex young people are inundated with in movies, in music, and on television.

"The whole point is, the world is absolutely seizing sexual languages and messages and images. Do you want the media defining how young people understand these terms or do you want guidance?" said Elizabeth Schroeder, the executive director of Answer, a program based at Rutgers University that provides and promotes sexuality education to students and educators.

Replacing Hodgepodge

The groups that crafted the standards wanted to provide guidelines that could be used in place of the hodgepodge of sex education lessons schools use now.

Even in states that require sex education, "I don't believe there's any state that has any kind of accountability" about those lessons, Ms. Schroeder said. "You really don't know what's being taught in the classroom."

But Peter Sprigg, a senior fellow for policy studies at the Family Research Council, in Washington, said decisions about the content of sex education shouldn't be made at the national level.

"The kind of sex ed you get in the inner city in D.C. will be quite different than the children get in rural North Dakota," Mr. Sprigg said. "They're all physically developing the same, but they're not all developing in the same cultural context."

His organization, which opposes abortion, also takes issue with specific parts of the standards, including information about emergency contraception and the message that homosexuality should be accepted.

While the standards do discuss abstinence as a choice, Mr. Sprigg said they don't go far enough in emphasizing it is the only 100-percent-effective way to avoid pregnancy or sexually transmitted diseases.

"They speak of abstinence as if it's just another contraceptive item: Use a condom, use a pill, or abstinence, which I felt kind of trivialized it," he said.

For Further Discussion

1. Given the lack of actual details from Shakespeare's life, how much can we infer about his sexuality? Is it justified to extrapolate life events based on the information in his fictional works of art? See the viewpoint by Stanley Wells to inform your answer.
2. Is *A Midsummer Night's Dream* as sexually explicit as many critics have suggested, or are they overanalyzing the work? See viewpoints by Deborah Baker Wyrick and Bruce Boehrer to inform your answer.
3. Is *A Midsummer Night's Dream* a work that empowers female sexuality, or does it suggest that women's needs are subordinate to those of the male characters? See viewpoints by Diane Elizabeth Dreher and Shirley Nelson Garner to inform your answer.
4. After reading the viewpoint by Deborah Baker Wyrick, discuss the importance of the scenes between Bottom as a donkey and the fairy queen, Titania. Is their interaction supposed to be viewed as an explicitly sexual romp, or as an innocent parody of the main male-female relationships, particularly that of Theseus and Hippolyta?
5. How have performances of *A Midsummer Night's Dream* changed with regard to sexuality since Shakespeare's own day? Are newer, less traditional versions more or less faithful to Shakespeare's original script? See the viewpoint by W. Reginald Rampone Jr. to inform your answer.
6. Is it appropriate to view all humans as either male or female, heterosexual or homosexual, or are there shades of gray in every sexual situation? See viewpoints by Apoorva Dutt and Eric Jaffe to inform your answer.

For Further Reading

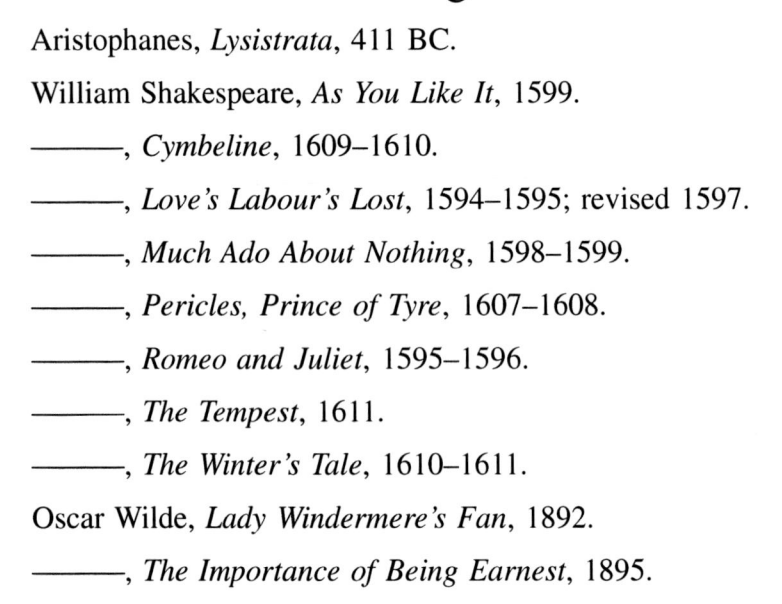

Aristophanes, *Lysistrata*, 411 BC.

William Shakespeare, *As You Like It*, 1599.

———, *Cymbeline*, 1609–1610.

———, *Love's Labour's Lost*, 1594–1595; revised 1597.

———, *Much Ado About Nothing*, 1598–1599.

———, *Pericles, Prince of Tyre*, 1607–1608.

———, *Romeo and Juliet*, 1595–1596.

———, *The Tempest*, 1611.

———, *The Winter's Tale*, 1610–1611.

Oscar Wilde, *Lady Windermere's Fan*, 1892.

———, *The Importance of Being Earnest*, 1895.

Bibliography

Books

John Atkins	*Sex in Literature.* London: Calder & Boyars, 1970.
David M. Bevington, ed.	*The Necessary Shakespeare.* New York: Longman, 2002.
Alan Bold, ed.	*The Sexual Dimension in Literature.* London: Vision Press, 1983.
Joseph Bristow	*Sexuality.* New York: Routledge, 2011.
James M. Bromley	*Intimacy and Sexuality in the Age of Shakespeare.* New York: Cambridge University Press, 2011.
E.A.M. Colman	*The Dramatic Use of Bawdy in Shakespeare.* London: Longman, 1974.
Jill Dolan	*Presence and Desire: Essays on Gender, Sexuality, Performance.* Ann Arbor: University of Michigan Press, 1993.
Jill Dolan	*Theatre & Sexuality.* New York: Palgrave Macmillan, 2010.
Evelyn Gajowski, ed.	*Presentism, Gender, and Sexuality in Shakespeare.* New York: Palgrave Macmillan, 2009.
Carolyn Ruth Swift Lenz, Gayle Greene, and Carol Thomas Neely, eds.	*The Woman's Part: Feminist Criticism of Shakespeare.* Urbana: University of Illinois Press, 1980.

Carole Levin and Karen Robertson, eds.	*Sexuality and Politics in Renaissance Drama.* Lewiston, NY: E. Mellen Press, 1991.
Madhavi Menon	*Wanton Words: Rhetoric and Sexuality in English Renaissance Drama.* Toronto: University of Toronto Press, 2004.
Véronique Mottier	*Sexuality.* New York: Sterling, 2010.
Timothy Murray	*Drama Trauma: Specters of Race and Sexuality in Performance, Video, and Art.* London: Routledge, 1997.
Marianne Novy	*Love's Argument: Gender Relations in Shakespeare.* Chapel Hill: University of North Carolina Press, 1984.
Robert A. Nye, ed.	*Sexuality.* Oxford, England: Oxford University Press, 1999.
James Redmond, ed.	*Drama, Sex and Politics.* Cambridge, England: Cambridge University Press, 1985.
Mary Beth Rose	*The Expense of Spirit: Love and Sexuality in English Renaissance Drama.* Ithaca, NY: Cornell University Press, 1988.
Valerie Traub	*Desire and Anxiety: Circulations of Sexuality in Shakespearean Drama.* London: Routledge, 1992.
Jeffrey Weeks	*Sexuality.* New York: Routledge, 2009.

Stanley Wells — *Looking for Sex in Shakespeare.* Cambridge, England: Cambridge University Press, 2004.

Periodicals

Laurie Abraham — "Teaching Good Sex," *New York Times Magazine*, November 16, 2011.

Katherine Angel — "Desire That Dare Not Speak," *New Statesman*, September 20, 2012.

Bruce Thomas Boehrer — "Bestial Buggery in *A Midsummer Night's Dream*," in *The Production of English Renaissance Culture.* Eds. David Lee Miller, Sharon O'Dair, and Harold Weber. Ithaca, NY: Cornell University Press, 1994.

Heather D. Boonstra — "Progressive and Pragmatic: The National Sexuality Education Standards for U.S. Public Schools," *Guttmacher Policy Review*, vol. 15, no. 2, Spring 2012.

John Russell Brown — "Representing Sexuality in Shakespeare's Plays," *New Theatre Quarterly: NTQ*, vol. 13, no. 51, August 1997.

Stephen M. Buhler — "Textual and Sexual Anxieties in Michael Hoffman's Film of *A Midsummer Night's Dream*," *Shakespeare Bulletin*, vol. 22, no. 3, Fall 2004.

Jean E. Howard	"Feminist Criticism," in *Shakespeare: An Oxford Guide*. Eds. Stanley Wells and Lena Cowen Orlin. New York: Oxford University Press, 2003.
Skiles Howard	"Hands, Feet, and Bottoms: Decentering the Cosmic Dance in *A Midsummer Night's Dream*," *Shakespeare Quarterly*, vol. 44, no. 3, Autumn 1993.
Richard Paul Knowles	"From *Dream* to Machine: Peter Brook, Robert Lepage, and the Contemporary Shakespearean Director as (Post) Modernist," *Theatre Journal*, vol. 50, no. 2, May 1998.
Louis Adrian Montrose	"'Shaping Fantasies': Figurations of Gender and Power in Elizabethan Culture," *Representations*, vol. 1, no. 2, Spring 1983.
Paul A. Olson	"*A Midsummer Night's Dream* and the Meaning of Court Marriage," *ELH*, vol. 24, no. 2, June 1957.
Peggy Orenstein	"The Way We Live Now: Playing at Sexy," *New York Times Magazine*, June 11, 2010.
Shombit Sengupta	"Creativity Loves Gays," *Financial Express*, June 3, 2012.
Lisa Taddeo	"Why We Cheat: An Honest Appraisal," *Esquire*, March 22, 2012.

Lisa Tremblay	"Porn Again: Why It's Time to Take Another Look at a Divisive Issue," *Herizons*, vol. 24, no. 3, Winter 2011.
Stanley Wells	"*A Midsummer Night's Dream* Revisited," *Critical Survey*, vol. 3, no. 1, 1991.

Index

A

Abstinence
    global trends, 141, 143–144
    purity rings and chastity vows, 141, 143, *144*
    sex education programs, 168, 169, 171, *172*, 173, 174
    See also Celibacy
Abuse in *The Comedy of Errors*, 69, 72–73
Ackerman, Joshua, 159–160
Actor's Workshop (San Francisco, CA), 10, 114
Admirable ass, 63, 76, 79–80, 82
Adolescent sexuality is a universal concern, 141–145
Adriana *(The Comedy of Errors)*, 69, 70, 73
Adultery. *See* Infidelity
Advertising and sex, 166
Advocates for Youth, 170, 171, 173
Aelian, 93
Aemilia *(The Comedy of Errors)*, 74–75
Aesop, 65
Africa
    abstinence rates, 143
    adolescent sexual activity, 142, 144–145
    AIDS/HIV, 143
    female body preferences, 154
    female genital mutilation, 143
AIDS, 143
Aishwarya (Indian gay woman), 146, 148–149
Alleyn, Edward, 42

All's Well That Ends Well (Shakespeare), 27
Alterity, 92, 93, 95
Amazons
    association with horses, 92
    Elizabeth I as, 52
    Hippolyta as, 51, 92, 115–116
    Titania as, 51–52
    women's independence and, 52
American Association for Health Education, 170
American School Health Association, 170
Americans. *See* United States
Anagnorisis, 104
Androgyny
    aristocracy and fashion, 35
    Hippolyta, 11, 107, 116
Angelo *(Measure for Measure)*, 27
Angelo *(The Comedy of Errors)*, 73
Answer, 170, 171, 173–174
Antipholus of Ephesus *(The Comedy of Errors)*, 69, 72–74
Antipholus of Syracuse *(The Comedy of Errors)*, 69–73
Antony and Cleopatra (Shakespeare), 29
Anxiety, sexual. *See* Fear of sexuality
Aphrodisiacs, 56
Apollo *(Metamorphoses)*, 65
Apollonian order, 62, 82
Apuleius, 67–68, 76
Arcadia (Sidney), 116
Arden, Mary, 21

Index

The Arden Edition of the Works of William Shakespeare: A Midsummer Night's Dream (Brooks), 48–49
Aristocracy
    androgynous fashions, 35
    arranged marriages, 60
Armenia, abstinence rates, 143
Artemis, Titania as, 51
    See also Diana
As You Like It (Shakespeare), 25, 54
Asia, adolescent contraception use, 144–145
Asinus portans mysteria, 65, 68, 75, 80
Ass motif
    The Comedy of Errors, 62, 68–75, 80
    A Midsummer Night's Dream, 62, 76–83, 133
    religious symbolism, 63–67, 74, 79
    sexual symbolism, 67–68, 69–70, 75, 76–78, 82, 93, 133
    term/linguistics, 62–63, 68, 78–79
    women as asses, 67, 69–70, 75
Asses' Feast, 64
Attractiveness, female, 153–157, 166
Authority
    male authority in *AMND*, 92, 94–95, 107–125
    parents as, 99
    See also Patriarchy
Autobiographical elements in Shakespeare's sonnets, 24, 37–42

B

Balaam (ass), 63–64, 79
Bale, Christian, 136
Bate, Jonathan, 12, 13
Bath, England, 37
Beatrice *(Much Ado About Nothing)*, 25
Beaumont, Francis, 30
Beauty and the beast motif, 62, 76–78
Bell's Edition of Shakespeare's Plays, 129
Benedick *(Much Ado About Nothing)*, 25
Berowne *(Love's Labour's Lost)*, 124
"Bestial Buggery in A Midsummer Night's Dream" (Boehrer), 11
Bestiality
    1935 Max Reinhardt film, 131
    beauty and the beast motif, 62, 76–78
    taboo sexuality and anxiety about marriage, 11, 88, 92–94
Bevington, David, 11
Bible, asses in, 63–64
Birth control. *See* Contraception
Bisexuality. *See* Homosexuality; Homosociality
Bloom, Harold, 11–12
Boehrer, Bruce, 11, 88–96
Boethius, 65
Bosson, Jennifer, 162
Bottom *(A Midsummer Night's Dream)*
    as ass, 62, 76–83, 133
    as bridegroom, 56–57
    as comic everyman, 82

literal mindedness, 80, 82
sexuality, 12, 78, 91, 138
See also Titania and Bottom bower scene
Bower scene. See Titania and Bottom bower scene
Brabantio *(Othello)*, 103
Brant, Sebastian, 66–67
Briancon (folk character), 49
Brides
    AMND urges brides to the wedding bed, 53–61
    folklore, 49, 51
    Hermia as shrinking, 59
    Hippolyta as unwilling, 114
Briggs, Katherine, 50
Brook, Peter, 10–11, 12, 128, 132–134
Brooks, Harold F., 48–49
Buhler, Stephen, 136–137
Bullying, 170
Burbage, Richard, 13, 34–35

C

Cagney, James, 130, *135*, 138
Calderwood, James, 11
Camp in Propeller production, 139
Campion, Thomas, 55–56
Canterbury Tales (Chaucer), 56, 57
Caribbean, adolescent contraception use, 144–145
Casual sex study, 151–152, 162–163
Catholic Church and contraception, 165
CDC (Centers for Disease Control and Prevention), 172
Cecilius Felix, 64

Celibacy
    Hermia, 77, 89, 92, 100
    Titania, 51, 61, 110
    See also Abstinence
Centers for Disease Control and Prevention (CDC), 172
Chad, adolescent sexual activity, 142
Changeling boy *(A Midsummer Night's Dream)*
    descriptions of, 108–113
    homosexual imagery, 107, 108–111, 113
    as symbol of child leaving mother, 77, 110–111
    as symbol of patriarchal conflict, 47–48, 95
    as symbol of procreation, 59–60
Chastity vows, 141, 143, *144*
Chaucer, Geoffrey, 56, 57, 65
Chick flicks, 161–162
Childhood
    changeling boy as symbol of child leaving mother, 77, 110–111
    rejection of by daughters, 97–98
Christ
    ass as symbol of, 64, 74
    as holy fool, 66
    imagery in *The Comedy of Errors*, 74
The Chronicles. See The Histories (Shakespeare)
Ciulei, Liviu, 10
Clark, Russell, 151–152, 162–163
Cloten *(Cymbeline)*, 104–105
Cobweb *(A Midsummer Night's Dream)*, 56
Codpieces, 10

Index

Collins, Jane, 139
The Comedies (Shakespeare)
    early, 22–23
    Lord Chamberlain's Men, 25
    parallels with the tragedies, 96
The Comedy of Errors (Shakespeare)
    ass motif, 62, 68–75
    as first play, 22
Commitment, men's desire for, 158–161
Condoms, 144
    See also Contraception
Congo, female genital mutilation, 143
Conley, Terri, 163
Consumerism and sex, 166
Consummation
    AMND urges brides to the wedding bed, 53–61
    Theseus, 11, 13
Contraception
    adolescent use of, 143, 144–145
    emergency, 170, 174
    national sex education standards are controversial, 169–174
    opposition, 164–165, 167
Coriolanus (Shakespeare), 29
Costuming
    codpieces, 10
    Hippolyta, 114
    men as women, 116, 138–139
    nudity, 10, 131, 137
    Oberon, 131
    Titania, 10, 131
    women as men, 116
Council of Chief State School Officers, 172
Courtship, absence of in *AMND*, 54
Craig, Gordon, 130
Crisis of intimacy, 97–98
Cross-dressing, 116, 147
Cross-species eroticism. *See* Bestiality
Cupid *(The Golden Ass)*, 76
Cymbeline (Shakespeare), 30, 104–105

D

Daly, Augustin, 129–130
"Dark lady" sonnets, 24, 39–42
Dash, Irene, 103
Daughters. *See* Fathers and daughters
Dauphine (folk character), 49
de Havilland, Olivia, 130, *135*
Defiance
    Shakespeare's defiant daughters affirm a new morality, 97–106
    of women and *AMND* as war between the sexes, 47–52
Demetrius *(A Midsummer Night's Dream)*
    codpiece, 10
    conflict with Helena, 48, 92, 122
    Egeus' desire for, 116, 118–119
    friendship with Lysander, 121–122
    ordeal in woods and becoming an adult, 101
    parallels with Titania and Bottom's bower scene, 81
    sexuality in Peter Brook production, 133

Democratic Republic of Congo, female genital mutilation, 143
Dench, Judi, 10, 131
Denmark, female body preferences, 155
Dependence. *See* Independence, women's
Desdemona *(Othello)*, 101, 103
Diana
    bridal fears and, 61
    Titania as, 51, 61
A Dictionary of Fairies (Briggs), 50
Dieterle, William, 130–131, 138
Dionysus, 62, 82
Disorder, Dionysian, 62, 82
Dogberry *(Much Ado About Nothing)*, 79
Dogs, 92, 122
Donne, John, 53, 54
Dreher, Diane Elisabeth, 97–106
Drew, John, 129
Dromio of Ephesus *(The Comedy of Errors)*, 69–75, 80
Dromio of Syracuse *(The Comedy of Errors)*, 70, 71, 72–73, 75
Duncan, Isadora, 129
Duncan-Jones, Katherine, 35
Dutt, Apoorva, 146–150
Dynamic attractiveness, 155–156

E

Eastwick, Paul, 156–157
Economic class
    adolescent contraception use, 145
    female body preferences, 155
Education
    adolescent contraception use and, 145
    sex education national standards are controversial, 169–174
    of Shakespeare, 21–22, 32–33
Edwardes, Jane, 136
Egeon *(The Comedy of Errors)*, 74–75
Egeus *(A Midsummer Night's Dream)*
    conflict with Hermia, 48, 92, 95, 97, 99–101
    homosexuality, 113, 116, 118–119
    Theseus' support, 90, 99–100, 114–115
Elizabeth I
    as Amazon, 52
    The Merry Wives of Windsor, 25
    portrait, *49*
Emergency contraception, 170, 174
England, Paula, 157–158
Epithalamion (Spenser), 54–55, 57–58, 59
"Epithalamion" (Wither), 55
Epithalamium, 53, 54–55, 57–60
Epstein, Alvin, 10, 12
Erasmus, 66
Erikson, Erik, 97–98
Eritrea, female genital mutilation, 143
Erotic literature in Shakespeare's education, 32–33
Erotophobia, 165–168
Ethiopia, abstinence rates, 143
Everett, Rupert, 136, 137
Extramarital affairs. *See* Infidelity

Index

F

Fairies
- campiness, 139
- eroticism in productions, 10
- names and sexual attributes, 56
- as symbols of groomsmen, 56

Falstaff
- *Henry IV* (Shakespeare), 25, 26, 35
- *The Merry Wives of Windsor*, 25

Family Research Council, 174

Fathers and daughters
- crisis of intimacy, 97–98
- *Cymbeline*, 103–104
- fathers as authority, 99
- Hermia and Egeus, 48, 90, 97, 99–101, 114, 116–119
- *The Merry Wives of Windsor*, 104, 105–106
- purity rings and chastity vows, 143, *144*
- *Romeo and Juliet*, 103–104
- Shakespeare's defiant daughters affirm a new morality, 97–106

Fear of sexuality
- Americans are not honest about sexuality, 164–168
- beauty and the beast motif, 62, 76–77
- brides, 57–59
- crisis of intimacy, 97–98
- Hermia, 59, 77, 133
- Theseus, 77

Fears of losing manhood, 162

Female genital mutilation, 141, 143–144

Fenton *(The Merry Wives of Windsor)*, 105–106

Fertility
- *AMND* as fertility rite, 107–108
- midsummer games and rituals, 48–49
- pre-Christian religions, 50, 51
- Titania as goddess of, 51
- wedding night and, 59–60
- and women's attractiveness, 153, 160

Filial obedience. *See* Fathers and daughters

Films
- 1999 Michael Hoffman production, 136–138
- 1968 Peter Hall production, 10, 12, 131–132
- 1935 Max Reinhardt production, 130–131, *135*, 138

Finkel, Eli, 156–157

First Folio (Shakespeare), 20, 31

Fletcher, John, 30

Florida State University sex study, 151–152

Flute *(A Midsummer Night's Dream)*, 91, 138

Folie (Erasmus), 66

Folios. *See First Folio* (Shakespeare)

Folklore and folk customs, 48–52

Fools
- ass as symbol, 64–68, 76, 78–79, 82
- wise, 83

Ford Foundation, 170

Forests of the Vampire: Slavic Myth (Phillips), 50–51

Frazer, James, 49, 51

Fussli, Johann Heinrich, 77

Future of sex education, 170, 171, 172

G

Gallun, Elizabeth, 172–173
Garner, Shirley Nelson, 107–123
Gataker, Thomas, 106
Gender identity and play-within-the-play, 91, 138
A General View of the Stage (Wilkes), 35
Gentleman, Francis, 129
George Gund Foundation, 170
Germany, infidelity study, 161
Gilligan, Carol, 98, 101
Globe Theater, 24–30
Godfrey, Derek, 131
The Golden Ass (Apuleius), 67–68, 76
The Golden Bough (Frazer), 49
Gouge, William, 106
Granville-Barker, Harley, 130
Gratiano *(The Merchant of Venice)*, 124
Greece, female body preferences, 155
Greenblatt, Stephen, 48
Greene, Robert, 22
Greer, Germaine, 35, 42
Grove Foundation, 170
Guthrie Theater (Minneapolis, MN), 10

H

"Haddington Masque" (Jonson), 59–60
Halio, Jay, 131, 133, 134
Hall, Edward, 138–139
Hall, John, 43
Hall, Peter, 10, 12, 131–132
Hall, Susanna. *See* Shakespeare, Susanna
Hamlet (Shakespeare), 25–26, 98
Hancock, John, 10
Harris, Richard Jackson, 161–162
Hartford Stage Company (CT), 10
Hatfield, Elaine, 151–152, 162–163
Hathaway, Anne, 22, 33–34, 42
Hauser, Debra, 170, 173
Heiman, Julia, 160, 162
Helen of Troy, 115
Helena *(A Midsummer Night's Dream)*
  conflict with Demetrius, 48, 92, 122
  ordeal in woods and becoming an adult, 101
  parallels with Titania and Bottom's bower scene, 81
  relationship with Hermia, 89–90, 119–123, 137
  sexual anxiety, 77, 133
Henry IV (Shakespeare), 25, 26
Henry V (Shakespeare), 26
Henry VI (Shakespeare), 23
Henry VIII (Shakespeare), 30–31
The Herbal Bed (Whelan), 43
Hermia *(A Midsummer Night's Dream)*
  celibacy, 77, 89, 92, 100
  defiance, 48, 90, 95, 97, 99–101
  ordeal in woods and becoming an adult, 101
  parallels with Titania and Bottom's bower scene, 81
  relationship with Helena, 89–90, 119–123, 137
  sexual anxiety, 59, 133
Herrick, Robert, 58–59, 60
Herzog, Dagmar, 165

Index

Hippolyta *(A Midsummer Night's Dream)*
    as Amazon, 51, 92, 115–116
    androgyny, 11, 107, 116
    association with horses, 92
    conflict with Theseus, 47, 51, 113–114, 131
Hirsch, John, 10
The Histories (Shakespeare)
    early, 23
    Lord Chamberlain's Men period, 26
HIV/AIDS, 143
Hoffman, Michael, 136–138
Holm, Ian, 131
Homosexuality
    AMND exposes taboo sexuality, 88–96
    boy actors and, 35
    changeling boy, 107, 108–111, 113
    critical readings, 11
    erotic literature in Shakespeare's education, 32–33
    fairies, 139
    Helena and Hermia, 89–90, 119–123
    Hippolyta, 11, 107
    labeling in India, 146–150
    Oberon, 110, 111, 113, 135–136
    play-within-a-play, 91, 137–138
    Puck, 135–136
    sex education, 174
    Shakespeare, William, 12–13, 41
    in sonnets, 40–41
    Theseus, 11, 113–116, 116
    See also Homosociality
Homosociality
    AMND exposes taboo sexuality, 88–96
    Helena and Hermia, 89–90, 119–123
    Hoffman film, 1999, 137–138
    Lysander and Demetrius, 121–122
    marriage threatens, 92–93, 94–96, 107
    suppression of women's, 110
    See also Homosexuality
Hooking up culture, 157–158
Horse imagery, 92, 93–94
Hourglass figure, 153
Huber, Valerie, 171
Humanism, 100
Humiliation, 94, 111–113
Hymen *(As You Like It)*, 54
Hymenaei (Jonson), 55, 57–58, 59

I

"I love you," saying, 159–160
Iago *(Othello)*, 28–29, 103
"If It Dries Out, It's No Good: Women, Hair and Rusalki Beliefs" (Rappaport), 50
Imogen *(Cymbeline)*, 104–105
Incest, 117, 170
Independence, women's
    attractiveness and body preferences, 155
    daughters and fathers, 101
    in folklore, 50–52
    Juliet, 103–104
India and sexual labels, 146–150
Indian boy. *See* Changeling boy *(A Midsummer Night's Dream)*
Infibulation, 143

See also Female genital mutilation

Infidelity
  The Comedy of Errors, 69
  Oberon and Titania, 77
  Othello, 28–29
  Quiney, Thomas, 44
  Shakespeare, Susanna, 43
  Shakespeare, William, 13, 32, 34, 39
  sonnets, 24, 39–42
  study of male and female perceptions, 161

Intimacy
  crisis of intimacy, 97–98
  nonsexual, 151, *158,* 160
  sex as primary means of, 166, 167

Isabella *(Measure for Measure),* 27

J

Jaffe, Eric, 151–163
James I, 27
January *(Canterbury Tales),* 56, 57
Jealousy
  The Comedy of Errors, 69
  Helena and Hermia, 121–122, 137
  Oberon, 110, 111–113
Jenine (Indian woman), 149–150
Jews, 64
Jonson, Ben, 53, 55, 57–58, 59–60
Jory, Victor, 130
Julia *(The Two Gentlemen of Verona),* 101–102
Juliet *(Romeo and Juliet),* 102, 103–104
Julius Caesar (Shakespeare), 25–26

K

Kean, Charles, 129
King John (Shakespeare), 26
King Lear (Shakespeare), 29, 36, 133
King of the Wood, 51
King's Men, 27–30
The Kinsey Institute, 160
Kline, Kevin, 136
Korngold, Erich Wolfgang, 130
Kott, Jan
  on fairies names, 56
  influence on productions of *AMND,* 10–12, 114, 128, 132–133
  Shakespeare Our Contemporary, 10, 132

L

Lamos, Mark, 10
Lane, John, 43
Lepage, Robert, 134–135, 136
Lesbians. *See* Homosexuality; Homosociality
LGBT. *See* Homosexuality; Homosociality
Little, Arthur L., Jr., 11
Long, Monique, 141–145
Lord Chamberlain's Men, 24–27
"Lord Hay's Masque" (Campion), 55–56
Louise, Anita, 130
Love, saying "I love you," 159–160
Love triangle in sonnets, 39–42
Love's Labour's Lost (Shakespeare)
  ass motif, 76
  ending, 53–54
  plot, 22–23
  women's friendships, 124

Index

Luciana *(The Comedy of Errors)*, 69, 70
Lucius *(The Golden Ass)*, 68, 76
Luddington, England, 34
Lyly, John, 79
Lysander *(A Midsummer Night's Dream)*
    friendship with Demetrius, 121–122
    ordeal in woods and becoming an adult, 101
    parallels with Titania and Bottom's bower scene, 81
    sexuality, 59, 133, 137

M

Macbeth (Shakespeare), 29
Mahendru, Karan, 146, 147–148
Malapropisms, 79, 81
Malone, Edward, 129
Maner, Jon, 161
Manhood, fear of losing, 162
Manningham, John, 13, 34
Marriage
    adolescent sexual activity and early, 142
    AMND urges brides to the wedding bed, 53–61
    anxiety about in *AMND*, 92, 94–96, 125
    arranged, 60
    Shakespeare, William, 22, 33–34
Marshall, David, 11
Masochism, 122
Masques, 53–54, 55
May Day and May games, 48–49, 58, 60
McGuire, Philip, 131

Measure for Measure (Shakespeare), 27, 36
Men
    adolescent sexual activity, 142
    AMND is a war between the sexes, 11, 47–52
    desire and, 151–163
    male authority in *AMND*, 92, 94–95, 107–125
    masculinity in play-within-the-play, 91
    women as sexual slaves in *AMND*, 69–70, 75, 101
Mendelssohn, Felix, 130, 131, 134
The Merchant of Venice (Shakespeare), 25, 124
"The Merchant's Tale" (Chaucer), 56, 57
The Merry Wives of Windsor (Shakespeare)
    defiant daughters, 104, 105–106
    Elizabeth I request, 25
    school imagery, 21
Metamorphoses (Ovid), 65
Metamorphosis
    ass motif in *AMND*, 76, 79, 80, 81
    ass motif in *The Comedy of Errors*, 70, 73, 75
    Ovid, 65
Midas, 65, 79, 81
Middle Temple (London), 34
Midsummer games and rituals, 48–49, 58–59
A Midsummer Night's Dream (Shakespeare)
    ass motif, 62, 76–83
    defiant daughters affirm a new morality in, 97, 99–101
    exposes taboo sexuality, 88–96

as Globe production, 25
is a war between the sexes, 47–52
is not a sexual play, 9–10, 12
productions have evolved, 128–139
submission of women, 107–125
urges brides to the wedding bed, 53–61
Miller, Saul, 161
Milton, John, 99
Minor, Bob, 164–168
Mirren, Helen, 131
Mississippi, sex education, 173
MIT, commitment study, 159–160
Mnouchkine, Ariane, 10
Mokosh (goddess of fertility), 50
Moriae Encomium (Erasmus), 66
Moth *(A Midsummer Night's Dream)*, 56
Much Ado About Nothing (Shakespeare), 25
Mud-wrestling in 1999 Michael Hoffman film, 137
Mustardseed *(A Midsummer Night's Dream)*, 56

N

Das Narrenschiff (Brant), 66–67
National Abstinence Education Association, 171
National Association of State Boards of Education, 172
National Education Association Health Information Network, 170
National Sexuality Education Standards, 169–174

Neeraj (Indian gay man), 146, 149–150
Neilson, Julia, 130
Nerissa *(The Merchant of Venice)*, 124
Netherlands, infidelity study, 161
Nevo, Ruth, 96
New Place (Stratford, England), 42, 43
Nick Bottom. See Bottom *(A Midsummer Night's Dream)*
Nobility. See Aristocracy
Noble, Adrian, 135–136
Nonsexual intimacy, 151, *158*, 160
Nudity
1999 Michael Hoffman film, 137
1968 Peter Hall film, 10, 131

O

Oberon *(A Midsummer Night's Dream)*
blessing, 123
conflict with Titania, 47–48, 59, 60, 108–111
Hall film, 1968, 131
homosexuality, 110, 111, 113, 135–136
infidelity, 77
jealousy, 110, 111–113
painting, *119*
On the Trail of the Women Warriors (Wilde), 51
Ophelia *(Hamlet)*, 98
Order, Apollonian, 62, 82
Othello (Shakespeare), 28–29, 101, 103
Th'Overthrow of Stage Plays (Rainolds), 35
Ovid, 65, 79

P

Page, Anne *(The Merry Wives of Windsor)*, 104, 105–106
Parallel Lives (Plutarch), 29
Parents. *See* Fathers and daughters
Partridge, Eric, 9
Patience, ass as symbol, 65, 70, 74
Patient Protection and Affordable Care Act (2010), 171
Paton, Joseph Noel, *119*
Patriarchy
    changeling boy as symbol of patriarchal conflict, 47–48, 95
    marriage threatens, 92–93, 94–96
    reestablishment of authority, 94–95, 107–125
    rejection by defiant daughters, 98
Peaseblossom *(A Midsummer Night's Dream)*, 56
Pepys, Samuel, 129
Pericles, Prince of Tyre (Shakespeare), 30, 36
Personality and attractiveness, 156–157
Pfeiffer, Michelle, 136
Pilkington, Ace G., 47–52
Pilkington, Olga A., 47–52
Dr. Pinch *(The Comedy of Errors)*, 74
Planché, James Robinson, 129
Plante, Rebecca, 157
Plautus *(The Comedy of Errors)*, 22
Play-within-the-play (*"Pyramus and Thisbe"*)
    Bottom's literal-mindedness, 80, 82
    homosociality in, 91, 137–138
Playboy Playmates, 155
Plutarch, 29, 64
Poel, William, 130
Poetry
    epithalamium, 53, 54–55, 57–60
    erotic literature in Shakespeare's education, 32–33
    The Rape of Lucrece, 23–24
    sonnets, 24, 37–42
    Venus and Adonis, 23–24
Portia *(The Merchant of Venice)*, 124
Portugal, female body preferences, 155
Posthumus *(Cymbeline)*, 104–105
Powell, Dick, 130, *135*
Pregnancy. *See* Contraception; Fertility
"Problem plays" (Shakespeare), 26–27
Productions of *A Midsummer Night's Dream*
    1999 film (Michael Hoffman), 136–138
    1968 film (Peter Hall), 10, 12, 131–132
    1935 film (Max Reinhardt), 130–131, *135*, 138
    all-male, 138–139
    Brook, Peter, 10–11, 12, 128, 132–134
    early, 128–129
    evolution of, 128–139
    focus on pageantry over sexuality, 9–10

focus on sexuality, 10–11, 128, 131–134
focus on spectacle *vs.* historical accuracy, 130–131
Kott, Jan influence, 10–12, 114, 128, 132–134
Lepage, Robert, 134–135, 136
modern, 132–139
19th century, 129–130
Noble, Adrian, 135–136
Propeller, 138–139
Propeller, 138–139
Prospero *(The Tempest),* 30
Prostitutes, 67
Proteus *(The Two Gentlemen of Verona),* 101–102
Psyche *(The Golden Ass),* 76
Puck *(A Midsummer Night's Dream)*
  bestial imagery, 92
  description of changeling boy, 108–111
  epilogue apology, 14
  as protector of marriage bed, 54–55
  sexuality, 134, 135–136
Puritans, 100, 101, 105, 106
Purity rings, 141, 143, *144*
"Pyramus and Thisbe" play-within-the-play
  Bottom's literal-mindedness, 80, 82
  homosociality in, 91, 137–138

Q

Quiney, Judith. *See* Shakespeare, Judith
Quiney, Richard, 43
Quiney, Shakespeare, 45
Quiney, Thomas, 43–44

R

Rainolds, John, 35
Rampone, W. Reginald, Jr., 128–139
Rape
  adolescent sexual activity, 142
  in *AMND,* 122, 131
  as separate from sex, 166
  sex education, 170
The Rape of Lucrece (Shakespeare), 23–24
Rappaport, Philippa, 50
Rehan, Ada, 129–130
Reinhardt, Max, 130–131, 138
Relationships
  AMND is a war between the sexes, 11, 47–52
  male desire for, 151, 152–153, 157–158, 160
  women as sexual slaves in *AMND,* 69–70, 75, 101
Religion
  ass as symbol, 63–64, 66
  fear of sexuality and contraception, 164–165
  folklore and folk customs, 48, 50
Reveille, 60–61
Revenge plays, 23
Richard II (Shakespeare), 26
Richard III (Shakespeare), 13, 23, 34–35
Rights
  sexual, 165
  women, 101
Ripa, Cesare, 66
Rockwell, Sam, 138
The Romances (Shakespeare), 30
Romantic comedy films, 161–162

Romeo and Juliet (Shakespeare), 25–26, *102*, 103–104
Rooney, Mickey, 130, *135*
Rothwell, Kenneth, 130–131
Royal National Theatre, 134–135
Royal Shakespeare Company productions
    Brook, Peter, 10–11, 12, 128, 132–134
    Noble, Adrian, 135–136
Rude mechanicals. *See* Bottom *(A Midsummer Night's Dream)*; Play-within-the-play *("Pyramus and Thisbe")*
Rusalka, 50–51

S

Same-sex relationships. *See* Homosexuality; Homosociality
Santorum, Rick, 164–165
Scandals in Shakespeare's family, 42–44
Schroeder, Elizabeth, 173–174
Selbourne, David, 134
Senegal, abstinence rates, 143
Sex in Crisis: The New Sexual Revolution and the Future of American Politics (Herzog), 165
Sexting, 170
Sexual abuse and sex education, 170
Sexual education standards are controversial, national, 169–174
Sexual harassment and sex education, 170
Sexuality
    adolescent sexuality is a universal concern, 141–145
    All's Well That Ends Well, 27
    Americans' dishonesty, 164–168
    AMND and women as sexual slaves, 69–70, 75, 101
    AMND exposes taboo sexuality, 88–96
    AMND is a war between the sexes, 47–52
    AMND is not a sexual play, 9–10, 12
    AMND urges brides to the wedding bed, 53–61
    male sexuality is complicated, 151–163
    national sex education standards are controversial, 169–174
    of Shakespeare himself, 12–13, 32, 37–42
    See also Homosexuality
Sexuality Information and Education Council of the United States (SIECUS), 170, 171
Sexually transmitted diseases (STDs)
    abstinence and, 143
    sex education and, 173
    Shakespeare, 32, 35
    Shakespeare's writing about, 35–37
Shah, Nirvi, 169–174
Shakespeare, Anne. *See* Hathaway, Anne
Shakespeare, Hamnet, 22, 34
Shakespeare, John, 21
Shakespeare, Judith, 22, 34, 43–45
Shakespeare, Mary, 21
Shakespeare, Susanna, 22, 34, 43, 44
Shakespeare: The Invention of the Human (Bloom), 11–12

Shakespeare, William
  biography, 20–31
  career, 22–30
  death, 30, 35
  education, 21–22
  infidelity, 13, 32, 34, 39
  marriage, 22, 33–34
  poetry, 21, 23–24, 37–42
  portrait, 28
  retirement, 30
  sexuality and sexual knowledge, 12–13, 32–45
  will, 44
Shakespeare Our Contemporary (Kott), 10, 132
Shakespeare's Bawdy (Partridge), 9
Sidney, Philip, 116
SIECUS (Sexuality Information and Education Council of the United States), 170, 171
Silvia (The Two Gentlemen of Verona), 101–102
Sinfield, Alan, 11
Size, and women's attractiveness, 153–154
Skinner, Otis, 129
Smith, Ralph, 43
Snout (A Midsummer Night's Dream), 138
Snug (A Midsummer Night's Dream), 91
Social class and adolescent contraception use, 145
Social media and sex education, 170
Society of State Leaders of Health and Physical Education, 170
Sonnet 35, 39
Sonnet 41, 39–40
Sonnet 93, 40
Sonnet 95, 40
Sonnet 96, 40
Sonnet 120, 40
Sonnet 129, 41–42
Sonnet 133, 40
Sonnet 134, 40
Sonnet 135, 40
Sonnet 137, 41
Sonnet 141, 41
Sonnet 142, 41
Sonnet 147, 41
Sonnet 152, 41
Sonnets
  autobiographical elements, 24, 37–42
  cover illustration, 38
Soul of the Age: A Biography of the Mind of William Shakespeare (Bate), 12
South Africa
  adolescent sexual activity, 142
  female body preferences, 154
Southampton, Earl of
  androgyny, 35
  Venus and Adonis and The Rape of Lucrece, 23–24
Spaniel imagery, 92, 122
Speed-dating, 156–157
Spenser, Edmund, 53, 54–55, 57–58, 59
Sprigg, Peter, 174
STDs. See Sexually transmitted diseases (STDs)
Stratford, England, 21–22, 30–31, 33
Stratford, Ontario, Canada, 10
Sub-Saharan Africa, adolescent sexual activity, 142

Index

Suffering
    ass as symbol, 63–64, 65, 74, 80
    Helena, 122–123
Supernatural and folk customs, 50
Swain, Lillian, 129–130
Swami, Viren, 154, 155–156
Sweden, midsummer celebrations, 49
Syphilis, 35–37

T

Taboo sexuality, *AMND* exposes, 88–96
Tacitus, 64
The Taming of the Shrew (Shakespeare), 25, 76
Teen sexuality is a universal concern, 141–145
The Tempest (Shakespeare), 30, 54
Temple Grafton, England, 34
Tertullian, 64
Texas, sex education, 173
Theseus *(A Midsummer Night's Dream)*
    conflict with Hermia, 48, 77, 90, 99–101, 114
    conflict with Hippolyta, 47, 51, 113–114, 131
    ducal authority, 95
    Hoffman film, 1999, 136–137
    sexuality, 11, 13, 113–116
Thisbe. *See* "Pyramus and Thisbe" play-within-the-play
Thorpe, Thomas, 42
Timon of Athens (Shakespeare), 29, 36
Titania *(A Midsummer Night's Dream)*
    blessing, 123
    conflict with Oberon, 47–48, 59, 60, 95, 108–111
    description of changeling boy, 108–111
    as goddess/Amazon, 51–52
    infidelity, 77
    paintings, *77, 119*
    sexuality, 10, 12, 78
    See also Titania and Bottom bower scene
Titania and Bottom bower scene
    beauty and the beast motif, 76–78
    bestiality imagery, 93–94, 133
    as comic axis of play, 80–81
    focus on humor over sexuality, 12, 77–78
    humiliation in, 112–113
    in 1935 Max Reinhardt production, 131
    parallels with lovers' scenes, 81
    as parody of wedding night, 53–61
    sexuality in 1999 Michael Hoffman film, 138
    sexuality in Peter Brooks' production, 10–11, 133, 134
    sexuality in Robert Lepage production, 134
Titania awakening (Fussli), *77*
Titus Andronicus (Shakespeare), 23
Tovee, Martin, 154
The Tragedies (Shakespeare)
    early, 23
    King's Men period, 27–30
    Lord Chamberlain's Men, 25–26
    parallels with the comedies, 96
Tree, Herbert Beerbohm, 130

Troilus and Cressida (Shakespeare), 27, 36
Twelfth Night (Shakespeare), 25, 34
Twins
    The Comedy of Errors (Shakespeare), 22
    Shakespeare, Judith and Hamnet, 22, 34
    Twelfth Night (Shakespeare), 25
The Two Gentlemen of Verona (Shakespeare), 22, 76, 101–102
The Two Noble Kinsmen (Shakespeare), 30–31

U

Unconscious in Adrian Noble production, 135–136
United Kingdom, female body preferences, 154, 155
United States
    abstinence pledges and use of contraception, 143
    Americans are not honest about sexuality, 164–168
    female body preferences, 155
    infidelity study, 161
    national sex education standards are controversial, 169–174
United States Agency for International Development (USAID), 143

V

Valentine (*The Two Gentlemen of Verona*), 101–102
Valeriano, Piero, 66
Vanity, ass as symbol, 65
Veneral disease. *See* Sexually transmitted diseases (STDs)
Venus and Adonis (Shakespeare), 23–24
Venus *(The Golden Ass)*, 76
Vestris, Lucia Elizabeth, 129
Vietnam, abstinence rates, 143
Violence
    The Comedy of Errors, 69, 72–73
    Kott, Jan, 10, 133
    Lepage production, 1992, 134
Virginity
    Amazons, 51
    AMND urges brides to the wedding bed, 53–61
    purity rings and chastity vows, 141, 143, *144*

W

Waist-to-hip ratio, 153, 155
Ward, Antony, 136
Warner Brothers, 130, *135*
Watermill Theatre (Bagnor Newbury, UK), 138–139
Wedding masque at end of *AMND*, 53–54
Weddings. *See* Consummation; Marriage
Wells, Alan, 9
Wells, Stanley, 12, 32–45
West, Dominic, 136
"W.H." dedication of sonnets, 24
Wheeler, Margaret, 44
Whelan, Peter, 43
Whitney, Geoffrey, 65–66
WHO (World Health Organization)

adolescent contraception use, 144–145
adolescent sexual behavior, 142
Wilde, Lyn Webster, 51
Wiles, David, 53–61
Wilkes, Thomas, 35
Will in the World: How Shakespeare Became Shakespeare (Greenblatt), 48
Williams, Gary Jay, 10
The Winter's Tale (Shakespeare), 30
Wisdom
  ass as symbol, 63, 76, 79–80, 82
  fools, 83
Wither, George, 55
Women
  adolescent sexual behavior, 142
  AMND is a war between the sexes, 11, 47–52
  animal imagery in *AMND*, 67, 69–70, 75, 92, 93–94, 122
  attractiveness, 153–155, 160
  beauty and the beast motif, 62, 76–78
  casual sex study, 151–152, 162–163
  control of sexuality, 167
  defiance in *AMND*, 47–52, 97–106
  female genital mutilation, 141
  independence, 50–52, 101, 155
  as sexual slaves in *AMND*, 69–70, 75, 101
  submission and suppression in *AMND*, 92, 107–125
  See also Fathers and daughters
World Health Organization (WHO)
  adolescent contraception use, 144–145
  adolescent sexual behavior, 142
Wyrick, Deborah Baker, 62–83

Y

Yale Repertory Theatre, 10, 12

Z

Zelmane *(Arcadia)*, 116
Zulu people, female body preferences, 154

CPSIA information can be obtained
at www.ICGtesting.com
Printed in the USA
FFOW02n0929130314
4257FF